HOW TO MAKE IT
IN A
MAN'S WORLD

*Best wishes
and good luck !*

Letty Pogrebin

How to make it
in a
man's world

BY

LETTY COTTIN POGREBIN

Doubleday & Company, Inc.

Garden City, New York

1970

For Bert

Contents

1.

What's in it for me?

A little boy is asked, "What do you want to be when you grow up?" He answers, "A daddy." His questioner is sure to pursue the issue: "Yes, but what do you want to *do?*" And the little fellow must come up with some occupational ambition— "I want to be a mailman" or "I want to take care of people's money on Wall Street" or "I want to draw comic strips like Daddy does."

A five-year-old girl is asked, "What do you want to be when you grow up?" She answers, "A mommy" and all the relatives are satisfied to leave it at that.

If this happened to you it should have been your first clue that it's a man's world. Little boys are given chemistry sets. Little girls are gifted with miniature ironing boards. High school boys are encouraged to take courses in economics, political science and physics. Their female classmates are reminded that "It's always wise to take typing so that you can have a skill to fall back on."

Even if a bright, ambitious girl goes to college, distinguishes herself academically and aims for a specific career or profession, she's likely to spend the first few years out of school convincing the makers of the man's world that she's not just marking time until somebody marries her. Basically, her problem stems from

the inescapable truth that people expect little girls to grow up
wanting to be a *mommy*.

Read "woman" for "mommy" and you have a capsule sum-
mary of the psychological albatross which has been swinging
around our necks for lo, these many years. How can we develop
our best selves if there is some onus upon being both a visceral
and a cerebral female? Remember the old arguments against
sending girls to college? "Does she need Tolstoy in the laundry
room? Calculus in the delivery room?" Breathes there a man
anywhere who would dare date himself with this archaic point
of view? Of course not.

Things have changed about educational opportunities for
women and it's time for the myths about women in a man's
world-at-large to be tossed into the same rubbish heap.

Are you hiding your brilliance under a mask of socially acceptable femininity? Do you feel slightly suspicious of successful
women—despite some gnawing envy of them? Are you afraid
to make your move into a challenging, stimulating more responsible job because of a vague fear that liking money is
masculine and enjoying power is a sign of penis envy?

Well, I'm here to tell you that it ain't necessarily so. A girl
can be brainy, accomplished, well salaried and highly motivated
in the world beyond college and apart from homemaking—and
still be *all* girl.

It's sexy to be competent. Not silly sexy, like perfume on
your kneecaps, but just downright attractive. A self-assured,
smart lady executive with a warm smile and a cool head can
run rings around a dewy-eyed dumb-dumb with a powder puff
for a brain. It's enchanting to be able *and* adorable. Ask any
really honest man. He'll have to admit that he likes having
clever, witty women around his nine-to-five domain. Not just
on the rungs below him but up there on the high wires. He'll
have to be truthful about how thoroughly appealing he finds

the impeccable, efficient girl in the next office who does the same job he does, as well as he does it.

If you're making less than $150 a week right now, if you're locked into an unsatisfying job that hasn't the foggiest hope of getting any better, if you're a glorified office wife watering the boss's begonia and chilling his martini, let's find out why.

Very possibly you've convinced yourself that the aunts and uncles were right. Good girls want to be mommies—and any other aspiration is suspect. If your unconscious is playing this trick on you—and you don't set matters right—you may very well type invoices and sharpen pencils until you can't even believe that you were voted most likely to succeed at Vassar. The fear of sacrificing femininity at the altar of success has kept thousands of girls "in their place." Is it *your* excuse, too? Are you a file clerk in an advertising agency because you love tall, dark and silent file cabinets? Or because you're afraid it's too *pushy* to suggest to your boss that a lipstick ad be done in day-glow colors on perfumed paper? Did it ever occur to you that he might need a brainstorm? Can you accept that he won't brand you masculine for volunteering it? He'll most likely crown you queen-for-the-day and yank you out of the file room on the spot!

So relax. You can be *you*—uncompromisingly feminine and true to yourself—and still be a little bit of a lady big shot in a man's world. It's perfectly all right to want to grow up to be a mommy *and* an advertising genius!

Don't let the "man's world" label scare you either. We have to call it by its rightful name because there are mostly men in it. But that doesn't mean you have to be mannish to join the club. You don't have to talk to a man in his own language. For a tough, straight-from-the-shoulder bull session or a salty cussing bout a guy can find a dozen takers in the executive men's room.

Forget about covering up your vulnerability or mastering your

female moodiness. Nobody expects a woman to be entirely un-
emotional or impervious to insult or coolly rational. No one
wants to ignore that you're a girl.

If you clear your mind of the platitudes and prejudices of
yesteryear you'll see in a jiffy that there's a place for you as a
woman and as a person in the big, wide, wonderful world of
business. Once and for all, let's torpedo the myth of the hard-
nosed, high-powered lady executive in the tailored brown suit,
complete with hairy legs, tight bun, pinched lips and sensible
walking shoes.

Today's girl-on-the-go doesn't talk like a sailor, walk like a
soldier or give orders like a marine. She's not butchy or prim.
She neither castrates the men in her life nor capitulates to them
mindlessly. She is likely to be securely feminine, well informed
in her field and the larger world around her, fashion conscious
and fetching, full of fascinating things to say and interested in an
infinite variety of subjects. Most of all, she is at home in the
world that moves and motivates men.

The absurd mannish myth character should by rights have
gone out with shoulder pads, running boards and chlorophyll
toothpaste. But the idea of the butch businesswoman is per-
petrated by two kinds of people: wives and husbands.

Wives need the comfortable, old-fashioned picture of the office
girl to still their fantasies of what their husbands do all day and
with whom. Women who cop out of the talent market to use
their sheepskin as a dish towel have persuaded themselves that
housewifery is synonymous with femininity and therefore business
ladies must all be dried-up old virgins with no breasts.

Husbands tenaciously cling to the myth for protection. The
longer it lasts, the longer their idyllic two-sided world can
remain sacrosanct. Husbands buttress the image of that neuter
population by coming home with tales of this sexless copywriter
and that old-maid personnel director, conveniently bypassing the

fact that the newest vice president of the firm bears a striking resemblance to Raquel Welch.

If you're comfortably, confidently feminine, if you're bright, eager and gracefully aggressive, it *can* mean that you're just the girl for the best of all possible worlds: business. Here, among the IBM typewriters, Xerox machines, time clocks, board rooms, mountains of carbon paper, coffee wagons, jangling telephones and wall-to-wall working people, you can find a warm niche and all the personal fulfillment a body can bear.

An ode to office life

Business and the office in which it is conducted can be the whole world in microcosm. All the specializations and professions, all the creative functions have their counterparts in some office somewhere.

If you aren't up to painting *The Last Supper* in oils, you can still do fashion illustrations, design product packages, draw cartoons, do advertising layouts, animate television commercials, paint *art nouveau* lettering for record album covers or design fabrics for the shower curtains of America.

If you don't think and write perfect, lucid sentences like Mary McCarthy, you can still have a terrific time writing speeches for front-line executives, composing lyrics for cereal jingles, writing press releases, creating verses for greeting cards or writing for news broadcasts.

The Actors Studio isn't pressing a scholarship upon you? So what! You needn't be an actress to be "in the theatre." There are lovely and lucrative *office* jobs to be had. You can negotiate movie contracts, you can be David Merrick's right-hand gal or become a press agent to a star. You can book road tours for a comedy team, manage an off-off-Broadway theatre or work as *Variety's* Las Vegas correspondent.

In business you can be both a Jill of all trades and a master of one. For example, you can know a smattering about enzymes and a smidgeon about duodenal ulcers. But you can still be a crackerjack editor of a popular medical monthly.

In business you can switch trains mid-journey and never get derailed. You may start as a receptionist, move into the art department and end up as something crazily unrelated—like sales manager for the entire West Coast territory or the wife of the chairman of the Board.

In business you can be a drudge one day, a duchess the next. You're not necessarily doomed if you join fifteen other girls in a training course for assistant buyers. Because if one of the top guns sends you to a wholesale house on a trial buying expedition for the store's boutique, and you corner the market on granny glasses before any other retail outlet in the city can get them on sale—then you might very well be given the Macy's Medal of Honor or the Korvette Croix de Guerre and a whopping promotion to boot.

In business it's the *people* who make the difference. The lady doctors and lawyers can depend on their training, and the lady writers and artists can ultimately count on their talent. But the lady in business has to turn to other people as often as she turns to her own inner resources. Happily for us all, other people in business are usually men. To be sure, girls are all over the lot. Every office is dripping with them as we will gloomily relate in a future chapter. But in the last analysis, we gals have to concede that it's a man's world. And to paraphrase the Big Bad Wolf: "All the better for making it, my dear."

If you're buying what I'm selling, then you have to be thoroughly convinced that the world of business is your scene, but you may still be forgiven for asking the classic question: What's in it for me?

In fact, after two or three years of executive bliss, just when you're sitting prettiest, you may detect some small inner voice murmuring still: "What was in it for me? What will be in it for me in the future?"

Introspection is the better part of valor

Partly, you ask the question because you're a woman and we women are congenital reason chasers. We find it next to impossible to want something without wanting to know why we want it.

Not inconsiderable, too, is the "image" problem. Betty Friedan dubbed it "The Feminine Mystique" at the same time that she began to beat the drums for the slow process of our emancipation. But we all retain a shadowy feeling of guilt if the office is more appealing than the kitchen, or if we prefer to brush the cobwebs from our minds instead of from the lampshades.

So you may be asking, "What's in it for me?" just to double-check your own motivation—that a spectacular job is not being used as a substitute for marriage, that making profits is not going to take the place of making babies.

Well, take it from one who's been through the mill. There's reassurance aplenty, whether you're a reason chaser or an image worrier.

Here's an introductory supply of reasons for the reason chaser who's not sure success is seemly. You want to make it in a man's world because these are the things you are *not—*

You're *not* afraid of success—and you're not afraid to admit it.

You're *not* averse to making lots of money—and you're not willing to concede any limitations on your potential salary.

You're *not* in a hurry to get married—but you don't view it as an either/or hang up.

You're *not* afraid to be called a career girl or a business-woman—in fact, you'd be rather proud of the designation.

And these are the things you *are*—

Excited at the prospect of using your mind and skills in a field that interests you.

Willing and eager to devote three to ten years to a specific career goal whether or not marriage is your main motto.

Honest enough to admit that you relish a little bit o' power and a whole lot of glamour and fun.

Fond of men, eager to meet them on their own ground *without* having to become "one of the boys."

Interested in broadening your horizons, meeting new people and justifying the time, trouble and trauma invested in your education.

Now for the image worriers I'll have to turn to my own thumbnail autobiographical sketch to provide reassurance. I'm not Paula Paragon-of-Perfection but if I could end up with both career and marriage/motherhood as compatible bedfellows—then so can you. Here are the vital statistics: Had three office jobs before graduating from college at age nineteen; had three more office jobs before joining present company; worked here six months before getting promotion to job I wanted most and still have today (in augmented form); took over this position at age

twenty-one (the boss thought I was twenty-three), but we'll get
to little white lies later); spent the following three years as a
career nut; married at age twenty-four, still working; gave birth
to twins at age twenty-five, still working; age twenty-eight now,
pregnant again at present writing and still working.

Given the above facts it may not surprise you to learn that I
think about image and The Feminine Mystique about as often
as I contemplate the wanderings of the planet Jupiter or the
second law of Thermodynamics.

About six out of every ten women executives that I meet are
leading "double" lives similar to or even more departmentalized
than my own. They also feel it no longer necessary to ask,
"What's in it for me" when surveying their careers. You can be
the same deep-down, real you whether your world focuses on
report cards or annual reports.

Nevertheless, the introspective query *is* natural when the
commitment to a career takes up most of a single girl's time and
energy. In the early stages you are not just doing something,
you're watching yourself do it; you're not just thinking about
something, you're thinking about why in the world you think
the way you do about that something. You're asking, "Who am
I?" and "Where am I going?"

Congratulations! You're not one of the contented cows. You
are simply being healthily analytical. You're big enough to as-
sess yourself, reach a judgment about your potential and act
upon it. If you've bought this book or rented it or borrowed it
from a friend, you've responded to the challenge in the book's
title. You've taken the first step out of line. Who wants to stay *in*
line? Who wants to be an orderly little soldier, content to follow
commands, slave over other people's detail work and plod home
uninspired and no more stimulated or enlightened than you
were the day before? There's a time to do a job for the glory

and the grandeur of somebody else and there's a time to say, "Hey, it's my turn."

If you feel that your turn has come, then throw away the rule book. You'll march to a different drummer and sometimes you'll hop and occasionally you'll skip and very often you'll jump —paces ahead of where you are *supposed* to be. Age is no limitation. Experience is something you'll measure not in years and months but in substance and content. The competition won't faze you. Six Radcliffe girls queued up for a position just means that the job is worth having.

If you're at all like me, you decided long ago that certain jobs are definitely *not* your cup of ambrosia. You adore the girl who waves a rat-tail comb like Leonard Bernstein waves a baton. But you'd never be a beautician. You'd give anything for the beautiful enunciation of that long-distance operator but Alexander Bell doesn't ring true as a career spot for you. You admire the girls who can talk to thirty children in some strange language called the New Math—but for all its rewards you know that teaching is not your calling.

For different reasons, you've already said "include me out" when it comes to the puristic performing or creative arts. If you weren't memorizing the parts of *all* the string instruments in Sibelius' Symphony No. One when you were seven years old, music may be something like a spectator sport for you.

Unless you were writing comparative literature theses on *Huckleberry Finn* and *The Divine Comedy* while all your friends were playing potsie, literature is something you read, not write.

You love to doodle shadow boxes and you're a regular Michelangelo when it comes to painting old wicker chairs. But an artist you aren't.

Acting probably appealed to you when all the action on

campus was going on behind the proscenium. But the roar of
the greasepaint only whispers to you now.

You're a realist about the specialties and the professions, too.
It would be thrilling to argue a miscegenation case before the
Supreme Court or assist at a historic heart transplant operation
or whip up a blueprint for a glittering suspension bridge across
the Long Island Sound—but you have neither the time nor the
inclination to crack the books for three or four more years after
you palm that bachelor's degree.

Lady lawyers, doctors, architects and engineers make up a
rarified elite group. They're fascinating friends and acquaintances. But because they're not you, don't jump to the conclusion that you're a no-talent wastrel whose education was a
stopgap between puberty and pregnancy.

I've gone through this process of elimination not to discourage
you but to assist you further in your search for "What's in it
for me?" By eliminating these unlikely areas of endeavor, you,
the business-world woman, can take a few welcome short cuts
through the jungles of introspection. Zero right in on your goal.
Abandon *guilt* all ye who enter Madison Avenue or Wall Street
or La Cienega Boulevard or Wabash Avenue or Main Street
U.S.A.

It's marvelous that you want to be another Geraldine Stutz
(president of Henri Bendel) or a duplicate Mary Wells (whose
advertising agency, Wells Rich Greene is the talk of the town)
or the next Muriel Siebert (first woman to hold a seat on the
New York Stock Exchange). These names are as hallowed in
some circles as Marie Curie's is in medical schools.

Before *your* name goes on the door and a rug goes on your
office floor you'll have to travel some portion of the picaresque
journey to the top with all the other typists and tigers. There
are unexpected forks in the road, hurdles that could never be
anticipated, misplaced signs and malicious people who are al-

ways popping out from behind a bush to give you the wrong directions. Be a good scout and be prepared for setbacks like the double-dealing double standard.

It exists all right, despite Title VII of the Civil Rights Act of 1964. Most firms pay lip service to gender blindness in hiring. Until June 25, 1969, the New York *Times* and other newspapers printed a notice such as this at the top of their classified pages:

> N.Y. State and City Laws Against Discrimination and the Federal Civil Rights Act of 1964 prohibit discrimination in employment because of sex unless based on a bona fide occupational qualification. Help Wanted and Situation Wanted Advertisements are arranged in columns captioned "Male & Female" for the convenience of readers and are not intended as an unlawful limitation or discrimination based on sex.

We can assume that a "bona fide occupational qualification" might be a good reason for placing an ad for an Armed Guard ($135 per week) in the male columns. But it doesn't quite explain why a listing for "Art Director $15–17,000" appeared only in the male section while the top offering under "Art" in the female columns on the same day was "Artist mech lrn design $125."

You *are* going to buck plenty of double-dealing double standard. But it is my recent observation that the glamour fields —advertising, book and magazine publishing, retailing, films, fashion and the like—seem to be dropping the barriers fastest, at least in hiring. Salaries are something else again.

I know that two editors who have worked for the same number of years for one publisher and who both have comparable work loads and responsibilities show a seventy-five-dollar-a-week difference in their paychecks. The male editor started at a slightly higher salary and his raises have been commensurately greater all along. A valid case can usually be made for the social justification of paying a family breadwinner at a better rate than one pays a woman who is supporting herself or supplementing her husband's income. However, you will probably not be in the mood for such fair-minded thinking if you find yourself in the same position as that female editor.

If you're the crusading kind you might want to consider challenging the neatly packaged socioeconomic excuse for the double standard in salaries. After all, the same boss who is so self-righteous about paying a man with four dependents fifty dollars extra for the same job isn't falling all over himself to right economic inequalities elsewhere in the firm. If he expects you to swallow his reasoning, he should be consistent. What about the janitor who has six children? Should he be earning one hundred dollars a week less than your male colleague who has only two children?

It's a knotty argument. Give the boss enough rope to explain himself and he'll surely hang himself on his half-baked logic. He couldn't sell the United States Congress; why should you have to buy it? But the law of the land and actual practice are two different facts of life. You may suffer from the cultural lag. Comfort yourself with the realization that seventy-five dollars per week won't mean *that* much to you when you're earning fifteen thousand dollars or upwards per year. There is still plenty of opportunity and monetary compensation in it for you, even if you do have to bow to the double standard here and there.

The myth of the husband-hunting paradise

Somehow the misconception has taken root that if a girl doesn't land a man during her college career she'll find him in her business career. Certainly, the magical machinations of a business day throw more men and women together more frequently than the champion matchmaker on a cruise ship could have believed possible in her wildest dreams. Friendships *do* blossom into courtships and love does lead to marriage. But it isn't a good rule of thumb to count on some automatic chemistry fomented at the water cooler and brought to a boil at the office Christmas party or the annual picnic.

There are no complex explanations for this. It's simply that most of the men at the water cooler are already married—just as any single girl over twenty-five will swear on her cashmere collection that most of the men *everywhere* are already married.

The older you become and the more successful, the more likely it is that you will meet older and more successful men who are, again, already married. This is no call for you to cast all aspirations to the wind. You can't remain a twenty-year-old file clerk forever just so that you will be appealing and accessible to the fresh-out-of-school unmarried male management trainees. It's a valiant, self-sacrifical thought. But you would surely tire of the young studs even before the job bored you to screams.

I am not, of course, claiming that your career climb is going to be devoid of occasional romantic interludes. Perish the thought. One of the obvious pleasures of making it, is making it. And there will be absolute armies of men providing escort all along the route.

But in analyzing dozens of friends' romantic case histories, a curious pattern has become clear to me. Girls who stay at the secretarial or clerical levels meet only the men in their own immediate offices, and often the marriageable pickings are slim. Whereas girls who move up to executive levels widen their scope of man-meeting so much that they are able to find husband material not so much through their job as *because* of what the job has made of them.

In other words, it's not *what* the girls do but, more essentially, *who* they have become. As a single girl executive, I dealt all day long with editors, newspaper reporters, motion-picture agents, book reviewers, authors, television and radio people, and publishing executives of every stripe. But I married a lawyer. I met him not at a sales conference or book convention but on Fire Island. Neither the man nor the place had the vaguest connection with my duties in book publishing.

Still, if my job had not entailed a thorough knowledge of publishing contracts, a dash of international copyright law, and some familiarity with legal terminology, I would not have been able to ask the question that started the conversation that started the courtship that led to the marriage. And if my job had not developed in me a strong streak of nerve, I would never have handed my business card to my future husband and said, "Would you call me Monday? I need some legal advice on a pending contract with a British publisher." In fact, if not for my job I would not have *had* a business card to give to him at all.

A good friend of mine met her husband through third-, fourth- and fifth-party intervention with only the most remote connection with her job. She is a designer of children's clothing. At a fall fashion showing, the mother of one of the child models asked the girl to design a one-of-a-kind, mother-daughter outfit for a society wedding. The girl delivered a smashing creation which managed to make the mother look seductive while the same dress on the daughter was bewitchingly innocent. The Park Avenue matron was so thrilled that, in addition to the fee, she invited the designer to the wedding.

During the cocktails and hors d'oeuvres at the reception, my friend met a charming gentleman who commended her for her own outfit. The girl thanked him and by way of making conversation, she related how she had come to be invited to the wedding in the first place. He was impressed with the mother/ daughter dresses. He was enchanted with the girl. But he was not the man she eventually married.

It seems he had this brother who was an independent film producer. And it just so happened that the brother had on the boards this low-budget film version of *Winnie-the-Pooh Meets Alice-in-Wonderland*. And naturally he needed children's costumes . . . and his brother just happened to be dating my friend the designer, who filled the bill. Final report: she was designing her own wedding dress.

The moral of both stories is that good prospects, like good fortune, often come from the most unexpected direction. If you concentrate on self-actualization, perfecting your performance on the job, acquiring knowledge and just creating a better you then you won't even notice that all your fellow hired hands are wearing plain gold bands on the ring finger.

If you want to make it in a man's world because you think it will help you make it to the altar, you may have another think coming. Helen Gurley Brown is past master at advising girls on sexy ways to meet men through a job. That's not my scene in this book. First of all, Helen has already captured all the medals on the subject in her books, *Sex and the Single Girl* and *Sex and the Office*. Secondly, I'm assuming that you've already read *her* books (partly because I devoted the better part of two years to publicizing them to runaway best-sellerdom). Finally, man-hunting is not my message because I conceive of "making it" as a matter of *self*-realization. *Your* progress is your most important product. Everything else follows from that.

If that strikes you as a self-centered, me-first point of view then let me phrase it more delicately: What enriches you enriches the company you work for. That was the motto of a model lady editor who gave a friend of mine her first news-

paper job. Sandi worked for the Tucson *Daily Citizen*. She had
a passionate interest in the art of making stained-glass windows.
The nearest place where a course was offered in stained-glass
workmanship was in Phoenix—120 miles away from Tucson.
Sandi's lady editor gave her one afternoon off each week so
that she could make the trip to Phoenix and back to take this
class.

Sandi is certain that the editor had nothing more than Sandi's
happiness in mind when she granted dispensation (with pay).
But as it turned out, Sandi wrote a fascinating feature story
on making stained-glass windows and the Tucson *Daily Citizen*
was credited with starting a sort of art renaissance in the city
because of this unusual piece of educational and cultural
journalism. What was good for Sandi was great for the *Citizen*.

I think that it's crucial to face facts about self-interest. It is
not a bad thing. Often, the actualization of your personal
goals and those of all the other individuals working with you
account for the intangible "spirit" that makes one company a
multimillion-dollar bonanza success while another company
plods along with mediocre profits.

When you sincerely feel that your name and your company's
name are linked together you'll see that mutual self-interest is
the healthiest form of symbiosis. You'll have to get pretty close
to the top-management ranks before you feel feverish when the
company catches a cold. But when that happens there's no
longer a "me" and a "they." There's just us. The speeches you
make, the books you write, the prizes you win—all of your
accomplishments will satisfy everyone else's self-interest too.

Obviously, "What's in it for me?" becomes an honest and
relevant question. It can be answered philosophically and specifi-
cally. The specifics are the most fun. For off in the promised
land of private offices untold pleasures lie in wait for today's
career woman. I've chosen several fields that are illustrative,

just to give you a mood picture of a typical workday in each. These are not fairy-tale days. These are once-over lightly but totally true profiles of average schedules in the lovely lives of women who *really* have something to wake up for every week-day morning.

Book publishing

Picture a day filled with brilliant authors, handsome pipe-smoking editors, tweedy book reviewers, sophisticated tele-vision producers, a smattering of supercelebrities, major money decisions made in the name of literature, negotiations with movie studios, lunch with a publisher from London, a think session with a Broadway producer looking for material.

Picture poolside autographing parties, introducing an author to Johnny Carson, celebrating a number-one best seller with a jeroboam of champagne on a boat trip around Manhattan Island; picture throwing a party for two hundred marvelous people—with somebody else's money, or traveling to Rome to get a manuscript from Roberto Rossellini, or charging a gorgeous wig on your expense account *for business purposes,* or reading about yourself and your favorite author in *Life* magazine.

A pipedream? Not at all! Every one of these things and better happened to me and to others I know.

I can't claim that my field or any of those described below offers one hundred per cent glamour. Even at the middle- and top-management levels there is inevitable drudgework. There *are* some chores that you can't assign to a secretary. What makes drudgework and routine tolerable is that as you progress in a job these things become less and less important; they occupy a shrinking portion of your time; they represent nothing more than a few bothersome moments of tedium in an other-

wise challenging day. Try to view drudgework as a motivation
for advancement and keep your eye on the sparrow of success.

Advertising

Imagine productive hours at your drawing board resulting in
the *perfect* package design, or meetings with clients who confidently place million-dollar accounts in your manicured hands,
or martinis at 12:30, 5:30 and 7:30—each with a different media
representative, or winning the year's most coveted copywriting
award. Imagine the case of scotch that arrives at your apartment, courtesy of an appreciative liquor account, or receiving
as a present that one-of-a-kind antique spice rack that you
hunted down as a prop for a television commercial. Imagine
watching the VIPs solicit new accounts by showing off your
layouts and bragging about *your* campaign for Fluffo Shaving
Cream; or junketing to Puerto Vallarta on the client's latest
model jet so that you can come home ten days later and
write with conviction about that glorious airplane; and imagine
picking up that incredible paycheck each week. It's no secret
that Mary Wells Lawrence pulls down a cool $225,000 a year.

A particularly nice feature about the advertising field is that
you can choose both the job and the industry. Just as there are
lawyers in law firms and lawyers who serve as house counsel
in every conceivable industry—so, too, there are advertising
agencies and then there are companies with advertising departments included in their own corporate setup. If you opt for
the agency, you can be a copywriter working on campaigns for
cereal, cigarettes, baby powder and beer. If you're employed
as advertising director within the beer company, your diversification is by function rather than product. You may do beer

copy, beer layouts, beer public relations, beer promotion and beer merchandising.

Advertising is a big, wide, wonderful world—and it's an open game for girls.

Television

How would you like your ideas and inspirations translated onto video tape each week to amuse, inform, provoke or pros-elytize the millions? How would you like to travel with your camera crew and staff to Haight-Ashbury in San Francisco or visit Timothy Leary's hideaway or live for two weeks with the East Village hippies, all for research and background on your one-hour special on "The LSD Generation?"

Or perhaps you would prefer to interview and select a panel of sparkling Hollywood celebrities for a discussion program on "The Death of the Star System." If not, you might enjoy working up a seminar of experimental biologists to probe advances in genetics. Or you might prefer to write scripts and play alter ego to a master of ceremonies known across the land. Or you *yourself* could go on camera with a five-minute feature segment during the "One O'Clock News" or interview taxi drivers during a strike. How would you like working with men, men, and more men—network men, cameramen, make-up men, advertising men. There's lots more to television than good ratings and solid sponsorship. There's a world behind the boob tube screen that might be just right for you.

A friend of mine does research for ABC-TV news documentaries. Another arranges for the big and little prizes on a quiz show. One girl just reads all the newspapers and magazines, clipping interesting or odd-ball news events so that the television personality she works for can use them in his repartee.

There are nearly as many jobs as there are commercials on prime time. And if you'll settle for audio without video, then radio broadcasting is just as wide open and with it.

The stock market

Here's a quick sketch of a customer's woman who believes that a brokerage house *can* be a home: She reads ticker tape like most women read a shopping list; she researches companies by getting to know their management, their earning power, their growth in sales and assets, their profit margins, their products, their degree of diversification, their prospects —and she *understands* it all; she handles absolute fortunes of other people's money—mostly men's—every day of the week; she addresses meetings of stock market experts and neophytes; her idea of a wacking good read is the annual report of the Ford Motor Company, her notion of a compelling conversation is a pro and con discussion of the Dow theory, her favorite off-duty pastime is plotting logarithmic charts of stock highs and lows.

She contributes a financial column to a syndicate servicing small-town newspapers. She always has something to say that any man in his right mind would like to hear: a stock tip. She has enough goodies in her own portfolio to guarantee that she can marry for love—not money!

Newspapers

Somewhere between *The Bobbsey Twins* and *The Fountainhead*, you probably got hooked on the adventures of Sandra Scoop, girl reporter from the *Morning Clarion* or the *Evening*

Breeze. She inevitably carried a shoulder bag as she jogged around Centreville in search of Truth. Remember?

By page 53, she had discovered a body buried behind the Old Mill. A hundred pages later, she had exposed the corrupt administrators at the state orphanage and a dozen pages after that, she had catalogued fifty examples of inhumane treatment of orphans. Three quarters of the way through the book she meets young Doctor Jim, romantic interest and orphanage reformer. Bango, smasho, goose pimples at the end when Girl Reporter and Doctor Jim solve the murder, she writes up the whole chilling story and he rehabilitates all the undernourished kiddies while marriage looms ahead. But first her next assignment. . . .

The newspaper business was my earliest obsession. I published my own monthly when I was nine years old. I can vouch for the irresistible attraction of print and columns, headlines and bylines and the delicious feeling that unseen subscribers may be breathlessly awaiting the next issue. From a marvelous little box of gelatin and some magical purple ink, I dutifully "published" a six-page newspaper—*The Zip Monthly* was its inspired masthead—and mailed it out to fifteen loyal subscribers.

A business prodigy I wasn't. A subscription cost friends and family thirty-six cents a year or three cents per copy. I then proceeded to mail each copy with a three-cent stamp (remember those?). That I never turned a profit seems to have been of no concern to me at all. Who needed any more reward than the crisp look of a well-planned page or the sweet pile of Letters to the Editor that accumulated each month?

I'm not suggesting that you rush off to the nearest hobby shop, buy a box of Hectograph duplicating gelatin and launch your own newspaper from one corner of the kitchen table. What I am suggesting is that you heed the voice of childhood fixation if you, too, were a newspaper nut.

What's in it for you? Here's a composite picture taken from the testimony of several girl reporters who have made it in this very tough man's field. The feature reporter for a big-city newspaper spent weeks making the rounds of swank, newly respectable bachelor/single girl bars for a special series on how boy meets girl the modern way. A drama-page reporter turned up the unsung heroine and the quiet hero in the world of ballet—the lady who makes those fluid costumes that a girl can dance in and the man whose toe shoes can be depended upon after hundreds of punishing pirouettes. A political-beat reporter covered the women's angle at the Republican convention. An enterprising girl wrote so many probing articles on real estate and architecture in her city that the editor gave her a column of her own every Sunday. Another girl goes to all the haute couture fashion shows from Pucci's palazzo in Florence to Rudi Gernreich's happenings on Seventh Avenue.

A black girl fresh from Columbia School of Journalism was the only one from her paper who was allowed into the Black Power conference. A lady football expert got an inside view of the social life of Joe Namath, Jets quarterback, and her sports story was a page-one feature. A New York *Post* girl reporter displayed Christmas cards from Senator Jacob Javits and Governor Nelson Rockefeller right beside the bud vase on her desk. A petite news photographer, weighted down by her Nikon, light meters and film bag, got a photographic scoop at a hippie wedding in Central Park.

These women are where the action is. And if you like fast-breaking news, if you like using a press card as an open sesame to the main scene in your city, if you like neat, accurate sentences, headlines that fit just so into two columns of space, deadlines, pressure, excitement, the clatter of wire-service machines and the much-heralded smell of printer's ink, then the fourth estate may well be your choice.

Motion pictures

There are girls I've heard about who start out as "gophers"
(they go for coffee or they go for sandwiches) and end up as
Academy Award-winning screenwriters. A script girl has been
known to work her way up to become a highly paid set decorator. There are little legends about such miracle workers in
the movie business. But the girls I know personally, both in
Hollywood and New York, have made it big off the movie set.
They're big deals who make big deals in the main office of
the studio or independent production company.

A story editor at M-G-M or Paramount or Embassy Pictures
is as important to the overall operation as a football scout is to
the Green Bay Packers. Without a scout's relentless scrutiny of
college lineman, a Jerry Kramer may never be recruited for
the team. And without a story editor's pursuit of properties,
movie production schedules would eventually grind to a halt.

My friends describe their jobs as a frenzied but fun-filled
round of lunches with agents and publishers, screenings, pre-
views, detective work (often bordering on spying) to determine
what the competition is up to and fascinating closed-door meetings about contract terms or policy decisions.

One story editor, who is almost blasé about her frequent
all-expenses-paid trips to the Coast, is nevertheless frankly awed
of a recent experience that her job made possible. Vladimir
Nabokov had decreed the method by which he would sell
motion-picture rights to his recent novel, *Ada*. He and his wife
would receive all emissaries of the movie companies at the
Nabokov home which is the Palace Hotel in Montreux, Switzer-
land. Each story editor or producer would be assigned a weekend
in which to read the nearly one thousand-page manuscript. No

copies of the manuscript would be circulated in the United
States.

My friend recalls her weekend as an unforgettable admixture
of pressure, fatigue, magnificent local scenery and conversations
with Mr. and Mrs. Nabokov that can only be termed rarified
intellectual discourses about the human condition. My friend
remembers feeling that seventy per cent of the conversations
went clear over her college-educated head. She remembers
reading hundreds of pages of Nabokov's manuscript each night
and feeling that most of *them* evaded her grasp.

The weekend left her with a good, strong sense of humility
and a bad case of exhaustion. But she wouldn't trade that
experience or the job that gave it to her for *all* the quiet jobs
back in her old home town.

Agencies

Name almost any creative or commercial endeavor and there
is most likely an agent firmly planted in the middle ground
where buyer and seller meet. The agent runs interference between the two parties with the best interests of her client
in her heart—and an objective appraisal of any given situation
at her fingertips.

Many of the top literary agents are women. They play a
curious range of roles, from pure professional to doting mother.
They read mountains of unsolicited manuscripts until they discover the writer with promise. They nurture him, encourage
him, reroute him, replot him and often edit him line by line
until he is ready to be unveiled. Then they submit his manuscript to a publisher along with a torrent of positive propaganda. They might present him as the new Norman Mailer or

as Appalachia's answer to John O'Hara—and they might be right.

And if they are right about tomorrow's talent, they'll ride right up to the top with him. Just as the theatrical agent will make the trip with her young actor or the model's agent with her hollow-cheeked beauty.

The agent who hits the jackpot with a talent or with a property doesn't owe it all to Dame Fortune. The agent and the dame are not really equal partners. It's the agent who does the work, has the fun and collects the ten per cent. She's the one who learns to trust her taste and instincts, who diligently pores over contracts, who charts a career or spawns a strategy. She's the girl who decides that for *her* the brightest spotlight shines on those in the wings.

Glamour fields galore

If none of these tempting professions satisfies your sweet tooth, you might find it mouth-watering to work in retailing or to be an interior decorator or a computer programmer or a bank president or dozens of other things in any of the glamour fields in the business world.

The point is—are you ready to make it big? Are the larger stakes attractive enough to you to justify a wholehearted commitment to meeting men on their home court and holding up your end of the game? Do you value your time, appreciate your abilities, expect more out of life than mere survival?

If you're shouting, "Yes, yes, yes!" then let's start getting down to cases. Now you know what you want. You can see yourself—beautiful, brainy, self-possessed, successful and still ultimately feminine. How do you get from here to there? The chapters ahead will try to lead the way.

2.

How to succeed in business without really typing

She couldn't let a broken toe slow down her job-hunting schedule. There were ninety other Radcliffe girls scanning the classified ads each day—every one of them desperate for any kind of editorial job in book publishing. With a Pappagallo pump on one foot and a pink satin bedroom slipper sheathing the bandage on the other, she limped into the office of the editor in chief.

"I know that pounding the pavements is a brutal business," he said smiling. "But haven't you overdone it?"

"I'm not *that* dedicated," she answered. "I'm just a casualty from a rugged East Hampton tennis game."

Their conversation proceeded like casual cocktail-party banter with nary a word about her typing skills or his company's benefits. Just as she was beginning to suspect that the editor needed a pal more than a secretary, he rose from his chair, thanked her for coming and asked her to write him a letter detailing why she wanted to work for him.

Out in the Fifth Avenue sunshine she checked her watch. This extraordinary noninterview had miraculously used up an hour and a half. She rushed home to write him his letter. But in view of the morning's warm, easygoing conversation she couldn't find the right tone. Should she play it straight, catalogue her credentials, enclose a resumé of college and summertime employment and cite her responsible nature or should she lay it on with more light, bouncy repartee? Neither of these tacks now seemed honest or appropriate. It would be disrespectful to come on as an old buddy (though she really felt like one). And it would be ludicrous to wax worshipful. She wanted to work for him with all her gut but she just couldn't play Jane Eyre to his Edward Rochester and get away with it.

She gave up. At least she viewed it as an exercise in futility when she wrote:

Dear Mr. Editor in Chief:
When we met I had only a broken toe. Now that you have given me my assignment I am completely paralyzed. You have made me feel as though I am nine years old again laboring in dancing class under the watchful eye of Miss Waldbaum.
Whenever we had "free expression" time I was the most creative little spirit in the class. But when Miss Waldbaum singled me out for an assignment and commanded, "Be a flower!" my leotard went limp.
By asking me to write this letter, you have asked me to be a flower.
Sincerely yours,

Mr. Editor in Chief was an exceptional man. His perspicacity was only exceeded by his good humor. He liked a good gamble. He hired her.

More than one way to toe the line

There are dozens of stories about the big break into the coveted field, working for the perfect boss and advancing to the ideal executive job. That story gets my vote as the kookiest and the most endearing. Its moral is worth emphasizing: One touch of originality and candor can be worth a thousand words of prosaic prose. But there are other girls who went about their career shopping in weird and way-out ways—each of which proves *something* about the personality quotient in business. Not everyone goes to secretarial school after college or crams down a six-week speedwriting course. The commandment is not chiseled in stone: Thou must fill out endless employment applications. Nor need you necessarily prepare yourself to be a file clerk for the first year, speak only when spoken to, wear white gloves or take what you're offered first time out.

The following job history bears as much resemblance to the broken-toe gal as a fig newton does to a petit four. Ann had no such luck on her first job out of college. After weeks of fruitless interviews she took a "temporary" job modeling in a coat-and-suit wholesale house. ("Is that a respectable job for a *cum laude?*" her mother moaned.)

There followed a picaresque journey through employment byways so diverse that the mind boggles: typist in the traffic department of an advertising agency; secretary to the director of a religious charity; sightseeing tour guide; research assistant to a famous New Deal historian; classified ad saleswoman for a skiing magazine.

At about this point, she suffered what may delicately be termed a crisis of identity. She was twenty-six. She was nobody going nowhere. There was only one honorable route left. She went back to school.

Two semesters at Columbia netted her a master's degree and the state's blessing "Go thou and teach the little children." But one semester of junior high school history convinced her that she had once again taken a wrong turn. She traded in the classroom for the kibbutz and the chalk dust for the dust storms of the Israeli Negev. A year had gone by before she felt she was ready to leave the Promised Land. She returned to New York a wordly wise but inwardly defeated young woman.

Nine years out of college, she found that she had made nine "wrong" life decisions—each one the elixir of the moment and each one horribly frustrating, wasteful or fruitless in the end. She was pushing thirty but she wasn't pushing any panic buttons. Not yet. She gave herself five months, until her thirtieth birthday, to find herself.

Dozens of interviews in different businesses filled the first month. Then one afternoon she met the director of a fellowship program. He needed an assistant to help him administer foundation funds to send worthy historians, researchers, archaeologists and artisans to Israel for a year's work/study fellowship. As he reviewed her resumé he fired questions at her: "Why didn't you stay with any of these jobs for longer than six months?" "Why did you choose Israel? "Why did you think you should teach history?" "Why did you work for the historian for so little salary?"

It all became clear to her as she parried his challenges. All her roving and job hopping had not been as aimless as it seemed. There *was* a pattern. And here was the very job that would make the frenetic pieces of the past nine years fall into place.

He hired her on the same hunch that made her take the job: that the foundation would offer her the ideal admixture of research, Israeli culture, involvement in history and the very real pleasure of travel back and forth to her second country.

She weathered her thirtieth birthday without so much as a light drizzle of tears. In fact, she has now been with the foundation for just over two years, and when I spoke to her last she couldn't stop blabbering about the Fellows and the fellows who made her life such a sheer treat.

Don't expect to have the first girl's colossal luck. To launch a job interview with a broken toe is literally to fall into a conversational gambit. But it had better be a real one. Limp or not, you are not likely to land the job of your dreams after your first interview—any more than you need fear floundering around for nine years as the wandering seeker did. Those were extremes. The average career expedition falls somewhere between the roller coaster and the slow boat to China.

If you start thinking about it early enough you can mastermind your own progress to a remarkable degree. Norman Vincent Pealish as it may sound, you *can* control your own destiny. What is required of you, I think, is a realistic appraisal of your talents and a steadfast attention to your goals. In other words, what can you do best, where do you want to do it and how much time will it take you to get there?

Damn the rule books, full speed ahead

You can find fifteen job manuals and fifty good friends who will counsel you to learn skills. "Before you take another step, take steno," they intone. "If you can type eighty words a minute, you can name your salary," is the pie-in-the-sky promise. But they don't mention that the sky has limits—somewhere around $150 a week—even if you can type the print off the keys of your IBM electric.

I stand ready to cite two $300-a-week "typeless" wage earners for every typing wizard that the secretarial schools point to with pride. The fact is that you're more apt to make it big and move up the executive ranks if you *aren't* a ninety-word-per-minute wonder. It stands to reason. Show me a boss who will let such a well-oiled secretarial machine out of his sight and I'll show you either a supremely selfless man or a complete idiot.

So unless your self-assessment has led you to categorize yourself as Supersecretary, you would be wise to view such manual skills as typing and steno as mere stepping stones. You may have to master the basics to get by or to get in—but don't allow yourself to become so proficient as a secretary or typist that you become indispensable at that one level.

Heresy? The nation's personnel directors may throw stones at me for undermining the foundations upon which every corporation is built. But I don't see those personnel directors hanging on for dear life to *their* secretarial jobs. The personnel bigwigs I've talked to think secretarial work is a glorious and important job—for somebody else.

They do have a point. About the vital role secretaries play in business and industry, I mean. When my secretary is on vacation or out sick for the day I realize full well that I become fifty per cent ineffectual. I can turn out the work by the basketful. But without Judy there to transcribe the dictaphone tape or dig out the past correspondence or take messages or coordinate all my projects, I become as ineffective as a man winking at a pretty girl from behind a closet door. There's action but no reaction.

So let's hear three cheers and a hallelujah for all the secretaries of the world. But let's not kid ourselves that becoming an A-1 secretary is a *professional* goal. That's why I call this chapter "How to succeed in business without really typing." There is a big difference between knowing how to type and *really* typing. And for a woman in a man's world, the longest, most arduous journey is from the cold steel typing table to the warm walnut desk of a lady executive. If you become too ensconced at the first, you may never get the chance to feel comfortable and cozy behind the second.

Don't for a minute think that the move can be made in one jump. I've never heard of a 97-pound weakling flouncing out

of her cap and gown and into the job of fashion coordinator
for I. Magnin. More often than not, a girl must be a patient
tenant on Secretarial Row before she can pass "Go" and
collect $200 a week or more. All I'm saying is, don't grow
roots. Don't build so many houses and hotels on that plot of
ground that you can't pull up stakes and move on at a moment's
notice.

Be incurably curious

While doing her time—typing without *really* typing and
taking dictation at a *sensible* rate—a girl should be reacting like
a seismograph to everything around her. What information is
on those royalty statements you've been typing since the tenth
of the month? Is the composer making more money from records
or sheet music? What percentage of the retail price of a book
does the author receive—and where does the rest go? How did
the mail-order advertising layout that you delivered to the
client last month pull in the way of cash orders? Who founded
your company and how long ago? What does a profit-and-loss
sheet look like? What's a self-liquidating premium? Which is
your company's main selling season? Most successful product?
Most lucrative territory?

As a secretary you can sponge up all the spilled information
that no one even realizes is trickling in your direction. Instead
of merely typing you can test your new-found knowledge as you
go. Read the incoming mail attentively. Be sure you understand everything referred to in an outgoing letter. Ask yourself
questions about forms. *Read* contracts as you fill in the provisions.
Ask your boss to explain technical terms. You're not being an
undercover Judas. You really will serve him better (though
for a shorter time) if you grasp the meaning behind all your
tasks, however menial.

At one book publishing house I did mountains of filing for the editorial department. Every report turned in by readers —no matter how inconsequential the manuscript—was tucked into the files. And what a ball I had reading not only the "to be filed" reports but the old and yellowed readers' reports from decades past. It was a major discovery when I unearthed a wispy sheet dated 1938 or '39. The reader had typed *Gone With the Wind* across the top of the page. The substance of the editorial opinion was: "This is a sprawling, endless ladies' novel set in the Civil War period. The characters are unreal, the dialogue is wooden and the plot is hopelessly involved. Suggest we pack it back into the crate in which it arrived and ship it home to the author, Southern housewife, Margaret Mitchell, who never should have bothered calculating the postage costs."

If my superiors, whether past or present, could have made such a monumental blunder, could it be that my own judgment might be just as good and valid as anyone else's?

The files of a company are a veritable cornucopia of information. You can follow one project from its inception to its completion right within the covers of one file folder. Chances are that you'll find it an instant education in the workings of your department or even a clue to the overall operation of the entire business. You may surprise yourself by coming up with silent suggestions for how something could have been accomplished even better. Those suggestions shouldn't stay silent for long.

What have you contributed lately?

Use those marvelously mediocre typing skills to bat out a memo on your own initiative. Offer your ideas for a window display. Comment on a proposal your boss may have been asked to consider. Practice couching your recommendations in modest language. Then your ideas become contributions to the firm, not criticisms of what is presently being done or implied attacks on someone else's inadequacy. The tired old platitude-cum-song title still packs a punch: it's not what you say, it's the way that you say it.

Pushy and Wrong	*Polite and Right*
"It makes no sense to introduce our do-it-yourself electronic mating/dating computer in November. Let's do a bang-up saturation campaign on it just before Valentine's Day. As it is, the ads have no zing."	"Our company's new dating computer is terrific. I especially like the fresh do-it-yourself concept because it puts some privacy back in romance. Suggestion: Why not launch our campaign Valentine's Day when thoughts automatically turn to love?—But I suppose we can't afford to hold it in reserve for three months."

Pushy alienates her superiors before they can even react to the merits of her suggestions. She has damned the existing plan and attacked the author of it. She assumes the stance of member of the team without anyone having invited her.

Polite opens from strength: with a sincere compliment for the product and acceptance of the campaign as it stands. Her suggestion as to the timing of its release is offered with low-key casualness and with an understanding of other considerations that may have dictated the decision to introduce the product in November. Polite has left the door open for her superior to say—with equal casualness—"Hey, you may have something there." If Polite's suggestion is rejected she won't be silenced forever. Her last sentence gives her superiors a graceful out: "Thanks for your idea about Valentine's Day but we can't afford to let the competition beat us to the market." Or "Your suggestion might have worked out fine but we must get this project on the books in the current fiscal year."

Pushy and Wrong	Polite and Right
"Why does this company persist in using old-fashioned lettering on its floor wax cans? This is the swinging seventies and Glisten Wax looks like it should be used on a 1935 floor. Let's update our image. Can't we do something about the design of that can? Maybe the agency that dreamed up the type face for Sparkle Wax could give us something contemporary too. I think 24-point Futura Bold Condensed type would be perfect."	"It's probably just a matter of individual taste, but I was struck by something I noticed in the supermarket yesterday. On the shelf containing floor waxes there were four brands in addition to Glisten, but Glisten was the hardest to spot. Could it be that our script lettering is more difficult to read than our competitors' bold block letters? Housewives have known the Glisten labels for thirty years so they probably have no difficulty recognizing our cans. But since I'm a new housewife I thought I would pass along my personal reaction for whatever it's worth."

Pushy is being insubordinate again. She's using jargon over her head; she's inviting a snub by issuing a challenge to the pros; what's worse she has praised the competition head on.

Polite is using simple psychology to best effect. By speaking of her personal reaction—as a consumer—she has made her criticism easy to swallow. After all, it's just one little shopper's point of view being passed along by a dutiful and concerned employee, who happens to be one and the same young woman. Nevertheless, her comment is a pretty serious indictment and she realizes it. So, again, she is careful to give her superiors the out. If they want to keep the product container looking dull and drab (suggesting that the product might do the same for a kitchen floor), then her boss can patiently explain to her that "you don't abandon a proven thirty-year-old trademark just to bend to popular whim."

Polite can still carry on business as usual in the company after her memo has been ignored or rejected. She hasn't given any of the higher-ups a corporate inferiority complex. It was only one gal's opinion. On the other hand, if her superiors are hip enough to recognize that it *is* time for a change, it's not unlikely that they will call in that bright young woman to see what change *she* may have in mind. When Polite finds herself seated at the conference table—not to take minutes but to give out with original thinking—her secretarial days are numbered.

Two examples do not a case history make. But I'll stop here because I am not suggesting that you remake yourself in the image of some polite paragon or that you memorize key phrases from some lexicon of model modesty. There is no rock-ribbed opening line with which to herald your debut out of the secretarial ranks and into the mainstream. You'll have to feel your way and gauge your boss's mood. You may decide that memos are too officious and that your man would be most receptive to an informal comment from you, delivered as casually as you deliver his mail. Or, if he's one of those meeting-mad, conference-crazy fellows who measures business productiveness by the number of hours filled in on his appointment pad, then do it his way. Secretaries *can* make appointments to confer with their own bosses.

Remember, too, that the man who receives a *written* suggestion is less likely to take sole credit for it, unconsciously or otherwise, than for one delivered in conversation.

Twenty questions—or even two hundred

If suggestions are one side of the coin, questions are the other. Abandon any ideas you may have about faking it during the early part of your career. You may be fooling some of the people some of the time, but you'll be cheating yourself all of the time if you try to pass off an understanding that you don't yet have. There's nothing wrong with asking questions —dozens of them or hundreds of them—until you have a full grasp of the business operation in your company.

Worrying about appearing dumb is just plain shortsighted. Every neophyte is a little bit dense at first. No one is going to rush to a hasty conclusion about your I.Q. just because you are inquisitive. Once you begin outthinking them, they'll assume you were smart all along. Others may be peeved at having to answer your questions all day long but I doubt that anyone will be annoyed enough to punish you by withholding information.

Pick your way through the pecking order

Whether you are asking bright questions, making recommendations or offering other services beyond the call of duty, remember that the object of your energies is to be chosen with care. If an aggressive, ambitious executive has been mucking up the machinery he may be on his way out. It would be futile to hitch your wagon to his waning star.

A clever girl I used to know was offered two routes out of the clerical department. She could be secretary to the editor in chief or secretary to the merchandising manager. She chose the latter. An alert, rational girl, my friend had heard gossip about the editor in chief. He was a respected, long-time employee but he was about to be involuntarily retired at the age of sixty-two. The merchandising manager, on the other hand, was thirty-four, brilliant, innovative, well-liked and rumored to be in line for a vice presidency. He was clearly the Young Turk in the firm. My girl friend was smart enough to join his departmental harem.

Figuring out the chemistry of any company may take five years. The interplay among departments may be the key. The executive pecking order always counts for a lot. A full comprehension of recent trends, triumphs and disasters will serve you somewhere along the line no matter how remote top-echelon policies may seem now. The job that is worth having is worth preparing for—in every way possible.

You can spout ideas like an automatic ice machine spouts cubes. You can be brimming with confidence, sopping up information about the business, charming the horn-rimmed glasses off your boss, performing your given tasks like a solid-gold genius. You can be thrilled with the field you've chosen to till and convinced that this is where you want to make your mark. You can be basking in compliments from the top brass and secure in your friendships with your peers. But with all that you may still be a have-not. How to make the executive leap —that is the question.

The main message is clear: *making it in a man's world* is your goal. *But*—getting there is half the fun. I've been sitting in my blue upholstered executive swivel chair for over eight years. Almost every day something exhilarating or exciting happens on my job. For each of those eight years my salary has gone up notches at a time. I've met or known a U. S. President (all right, a former President), a Member of British Parliament, a heavyweight champion of the world and a Marx brother or two. But, believe it or not, I remember most vividly those first two or three years in the job jungle when every knock had to be turned into a boost and when every unfamous friend or boss became a vital figure in my career history.

The sooner the better

The timing of your big break out of the rut is an arbitrary decision. But what's wrong with right now? In my case, early commitment made all the difference. For some reason—call it a love affair with the printed word—I knew as early as my high school days that I wanted to work in publishing. Naturally, I had no idea about the difference between publishing newspapers, books, magazines or racing forms. But I was determined to waste no time finding out.

The high school newspaper was my first introduction to the fourth estate. It happened to be an award-winning weekly with a professional ex-newspaperman as its faculty adviser. I was hooked. I learned to write a correct lead paragraph. I interviewed local candidates to the state Senate and the school's star athletes. I visited the printer, sweated over deadline stories, strained to write perfect New York *Times*-ish headlines that fit the column width to the last apostrophe. I was ready for the big time.

The summer that I graduated I was sixteen and eager to put in action my theories about planned careerhood. With working papers in hand I stormed the bastions of a small newspaper in upstate New York where my family was spending the summer. The first fall from innocence: nobody needed a sixteen-year-old for fifty dollars a week or even for fifty dollars for the whole summer. But for no pay at all, they would put up with me. I dubbed myself "apprentice journalist" and gratefully took my place at a spare desk in the women's news department.

Unless your family depends on your summer income to supplement your college costs, there's no reason why you shouldn't consider sacrificing income at the altar of experience. Certain companies simply cannot justify hiring young inexperienced kids for summer work. But from your point of view it's a tangible investment of three or four months into your future worth as an employable creature. The years will repay you.

Certainly it's preferable to earn while you learn. And in some fields that advertising come-on does prove to be true. In any case, let's agree that summers are valuable chunks of time and well worth using if you're still in the student category. You're not going to loaf around your parents' golf club or goof off in the guise of devoting the summer to the complete works of Charles Dickens. That's just a copout.

Unless you're planning to succeed Jennie Grossinger, you're not going to be a waitress in the Catskills either. Or zip off to Venice or follow some exchange student back to Paris for love's sake.

It isn't just a little vacation that you'd be frittering away. It's four months or one third of a year. After three working summers you can chalk up a year's experience before your classmates ever *see* a Social Security card.

Little bright lies

In order to land the kind of summer job that will look good on a resumé later and really teach you something now, you may have to practice the delicate art of deceit. Shrieks of protest usually greet my advice that girls *not* learn to type too well. But veritable *wails* can be expected whenever I tell people that the beginner must perjure or perish in the job-hunting game. I still stand by the pronouncement. You've got to lie like an inscrutable oriental rug.

Lie about your age by as many years as you feel you need to establish a patina of maturity. Just be sure that it's vaguely within reason. Your mirror and your good sense should be your guide. It would be foolish to exceed three or four years in this temporary deceit. You'd be sure to trip up on some detail of social or cultural familiarity. It happened to me even with my measly exaggeration of two years. (Social Security payoffs will come through to me at age sixty instead of sixty-two. When I applied for my card I said that I was nineteen when I was actually seventeen. Maybe that was going *too* far. I must get around to correcting the fib one of these days.)

I did just fine memorizing an earlier year of birth and boning up on Adlai Stevenson's candidacy, Johnny Ray records, the Hungarian Revolution of 1956 and other political and social events which wouldn't be quite so hazy if I really *were* two years older when I had lived through them. But I goofed once in an offhand television I.Q. test.

I *do* remember the early days of television—when Milton Berle could be seen Tuesday nights on a seven-inch screen, darkly through a thick glass magnifier. And I remember when Sid Caesar and Imogene Coca cavorted around "Your Show of Shows" every Saturday night. But in an office game of Trivia I flunked out completely.

If I had lived through these pop-culture experiences as an adult I would have been likely to remember the campy details. Because I was really a child viewer I remember only Berle's custard pies and Caesar's phony German accent.

Such slip-ups may happen, and they *are* momentarily embarrassing and they do prove that honesty is the best policy and all that. But it goes without saying that you're going to be basically honest about your essential qualities and abilities.

Now that I'm nudging thirty it seems ridiculous that I ever felt the need to pass for older. But as long as people persist in viewing a young woman as a "nineteen-year-old kid" instead of as a "person," age can be a handicap for the young as well

as for the senior citizen in the job market. There are pre-
conceptions that are prevalent among those on the "wrong" side
of the generation gap. These may militate against a nineteen-
year-old being hired to work with mature people. Whether a
personnel interviewer expects that you might smoke pot on the
job or wear hippie bells or steal paper clips depends on the
interviewer's individual concept of current youth. Unfortunately,
you are apt to be judged, somewhat at least, by whatever is the
going generalization about your contemporaries. Lying about
her age is a bright girl's only weapon when she wants to start
early in the competitive game of Making It. File under Little
Bright Lies—and forget.

Nonfelonious fibs

The same goes for the Future Plans Fib. If you're going to
use the summers between semesters to best advantage you may
find that available temporary jobs are too, too menial to be
worth your precious time. That may sound condescending.
But it can't be argued that licking envelopes all summer in a
mail-order house is ever going to expand your understanding
of the advertising field.

The Future Plans Fib goes into effect when you are applying
for a bona fide position on a presumably permanent basis. You
may have to swear on a stack of dictation pads that you have
quit college and that you are now completely career oriented.
Well-meaning businessmen will pressure you to return to school,
get your degree and then come knocking for a job. Don't
succumb to truth telling. If you admit that you're really only
planning to work for the summer but you want a good job for
those four months so that you will be better equipped for your
future, that kind man who was so interested in your college

degree will congratulate you on your good sense—and promptly
send you packing. He's no jerk. He knows the pattern: he'll
hire you, train you and just be getting to depend upon you
when you'll beat it back to Berkeley or Skidmore—and he'll have
to start all over again with someone else.

When you realize "It's either him or me" you may decide
that the Future Plans Fib is a necessary evil. And you may
be right. It worked for me—and as far as I can learn, none
of my bosses has failed to forgive me for my declarations of
being a dedicated college dropout. As a final rationalization,
you may find comfort in the fact that four months are not such
an unusual term of employment even for gals who are already
in the postgraduate job corps. So you needn't feel guilty when
you announce after Labor Day that the call of the campus is,
after all, irresistible.

While still in school, get a job for a few hours a week that
will give you *some* business experience, as closely related to
your goal as possible. Everyone should be able to tell an
invoice from a petty cash voucher—even philosophy majors.
It's important to be able to fill in those blanks labeled "Previous
Experience" when you apply for your first real job. "Part-
time typist in Admissions office" or "clerk at college bookstore"
looks better than "no business experience." And even ten hours
of work each week provides you with *someone* to give you that
all-important personal reference.

Better to be late than procrastinate

If you've been out from under the mortarboard cap for some
time it doesn't do any good to look wistfully back at lost
opportunities. Late bloomers are often the classiest plants in
the greenhouse. With your competent but *controlled* typing

and stenography skills and your dedicated curiosity about business methods and trade secrets you can decide to make your move even after years of vegetating. It's never too late. A stultifying job in a dull office is only a prison of your own making. It isn't a life sentence.

Don't look for clemency from your boss. If you've been wedged into a secretarial cell for ages, your boss has probably learned to think of himself as a benevolent and paternal warden. He's not likely to recommend you for parole—I mean promotion—no matter how blazingly you suddenly turn on the brilliance. The *only* way up is the way out. You've got to leave behind those profit-sharing goodies, those comfortable old pals and that gnawing *noblesse oblige*. You can always come back for a visit.

I have a friend whose tale can be an inspiration to anyone. She wanted to be a writer. But she feared that any job involving commercial writing would pollute her talent. So she looked for work as far afield of the literary Muse as possible. She became a key punch operator. The odd hours of employment suited her writing habits. The work required no creative output. All day long for nearly two years she punched holes in IBM cards, translating written information into computer language which could then be put onto magnetic tape the better to serve business and industry.

One night at a party she met a man whose innocent social queries changed her life.

"What do you do?" he said, as zillions of young men have asked zillions of young women at zillions of parties.

"I'm a writer," she answered.

"Oh? What have you published?" he countered.

"Nothing yet," she said. "I'm a struggling writer."

"Well then, you must do *something* for a living."

"I'm a key punch operator," she said. "But that's just to pay the bills."

"I'll bet you don't last six weeks at that brainless labor," he said brightly.

"Oh, no. I've been doing it for two years," she said. "It's not that bad."

He looked at her for some long moments. He was incredulous. And then she saw his interest in her fade away. Tangibly, visibly, he was tuning her out.

"What a way to spend a life," he said, slipping away in the direction of the liquor.

My friend said that those final words rang in her ears for days. She *was* spending her life—like a thoughtless heiress might fritter away a huge fortune. Inevitably she would bankrupt herself. In two years she hadn't written anything worth publishing or even worth submitting. But in those two years she had *become* a key punch operator—content at her machine, punching holes in cards and spending two thousand hours a year for two years of her lifetime.

She decided to stay with the computer field or Cybernetics as she now calls it. But she was ready to move into the man's world. She enrolled in a six-week course in programming given by a major oil company. While she learned to write programs and design systems she also learned that the average salary of a systems manager is fifteen thousand dollars. (That could buy a lot of typing ribbon for her Great American Novel!) She discovered that the computer field was so new that big opportunities were available to those with very little experience. She found out that this young industry couldn't afford to discriminate against women. They needed people too desperately.

Unexpectedly, she discovered an underground population of psychologists in the middle-management levels of the oil

company where she went for her first job. The men who
interviewed her explained with pride that psychologists were
the cornerstone of Cybernetics progress. Wherever people
feared that a computer would make their jobs obsolete, psychologists served to soften the blow; to propagandize as well
as to instruct the employees.

My friend had been a psychology major in college. The two
men who interviewed her admitted months later that they had
hired her because they wanted someone "to talk to at lunch."

She thrived at the oil company. But she had learned the
benefits of mobility. After eight months, she left to become
a programmer at an advertising agency. A year later she was
considered a specialist in programming for the problems and
needs unique to advertising agencies. Again, she changed jobs.
This time she was hired by one of the largest advertising
agencies in the country at a salary of that promised fifteen
thousand and with the title Senior Programmer. She was feeling
her electronic oats. She suggested that the agency program into
a computer all its media information so that a client could be
told *instantly* what are the rates for *Life, Look,* the Chicago
Tribune or any other publication in the country; how much
for a color page in *The New Yorker;* what's the advertising
deadline for the March issue of *Town and Country;* or the
regional breakdown for *Time*'s special editions.

My friend's computerized media operation couldn't help but
attract the awe and attention of the top executives. It made
everyone's job easier. It also brought her a five-thousand-dollar-
a-year raise and the title of Systems Analyst. Nearly two
years after the fateful conversation at that party she had
actually *quadrupled* her salary!

No, she still hasn't published any of her writing. But she
hadn't published as a key punch operator either.

Mobility plus agility equals success

Another girl—a true intellectual and seeker of wisdom—also puts a lot of stock in mobility. But her rationale is a philosophical one. "I always moved in the direction of my least knowledge," she says cryptically. "I had a secret desire to be the Renaissance Woman—to be wordly and practical, aware and resourceful, successful but never stagnant."

As befits such sentiments, this girl was a philosophy major. But the rest of her dossier defies definition. A philosophy major who wants to be an architect? A philosophy major who works summers for the *American Druggist* one year and as an arts and crafts counselor, the next? A philosophy major who refuses a job teaching philosophy at the University of Colorado and ends up as a newspaper reporter and columnist? It doesn't figure. But she wasn't out to make her life logical —and neither must you. She was out to experience life, contribute to something, learn everything she possibly could about anything that interested her, and somehow earn a salary in the process.

So she moved around. From the offbeat summer jobs to a flirtation with college teaching to a Western newspaper, writing features, to a big city Eastern newspaper where she was hired for a one-week trial period. Three months later she was still there. Union rules demanded that she either be released at this point or hired permanently. She was called to the publisher's office.

For twenty minutes they talked about the newspaper and the city and about auto racing and politics. It was 1964.

"If you had to interview Madame Nhu, what would you ask her?" the publisher inquired.

"I would ask whom she would support in the American presidential election. It would probably reveal more about her than ten direct questions might."

"And who would she say she was for, do you think?" asked the publisher.

"Goldwater," the girl answered.

She worked at this newspaper for four years. Because she kept moving within the confines of the newspaper she didn't feel she had to move out of it. Writing features was enough of an education to satisfy this girl's ravenous hunger for "conscious-expanding" experience. Whatever was on the feature editor's private mind surfaced in the form of an assignment for my friend.

When the editor's child went for a tonsilectomy, my friend was assigned to check out child psychologists and pediatricians for a feature entitled "How to Prepare Your Child for the Hospital."

When the editor moved into a new high-rise apartment, he was plagued by noise coming through the thin walls. Result: she wrote a feature, "How to Cut Down on the Noise in Your Life." She studied architect's plans for city housing developments, reported on the money saved by building plasterboard walls, interviewed residents of noise-afflicted apartments and suggested ten rules for a quieter life.

When the editor's wife joined a women's peace group, the girl was assigned to a series on women in the antiwar movement.

"They weren't always subjects that satisfied the Renaissance Woman in me," recalls my friend. "But the editor taught me something vital: if you're given a lemon, don't grimace. Make lemonade."

My own job mobility was based on a less noble motivation than that of my philosopher-journalist friend. I needed money.

After my apprentice summer on the upstate newspaper I moved my sights into the book publishing field. The salary potential seemed better and the jobs somehow more ladylike. (I wasn't tough enough for the newspaper business. I could lie about my age but I couldn't falsify my innocence. In those days I was easily shocked and upset—by murders, gambling raids, lost children, cursing in the office and three-alarm fires.)

I got my first job in publishing through the well-trod route of the employment agency. Fifty-five dollars a week, and in 1957 that seemed like a munificent clerical error. I worked for a dashing bearded man in the contracts and rights department of Simon & Schuster. That meant I could type onto forms the provisions of publishing agreements for such authors as Meyer Levin and Bertrand Russell. I could see how much the publisher was paying an author of a first novel as opposed to what Kay Thompson got for her classic *Eloise*. I could watch my boss negotiate for the sale of French publishing rights in a book after I had typed his letters "pitching" it to our literary agents in Paris.

That first summer at Simon & Schuster was the perfect chance introduction to the unseen skeleton that holds up the body of book publishing: what an author is paid to write a book and what others pay the publisher to *use* the book—as a movie, play, magazine serial or in foreign translation.

I was eighteen (passing for twenty) and I felt that I was invisible. Everyone was glamorous, sophisticated and confident. Every conversation that I overheard was witty and clever. Editors were sweeping past my desk with authors like Rona Jaffe or Sloan Wilson in tow. I kept my nose in the contract file and my eyes on everything. I knew I could never hope to be *of* these people, so I merely wanted to be *around* them. It was a glorious summer. I remember it best because of Rona Jaffe. It was the summer that her book *The Best of Everything*

became a best seller. How mystical, I thought, that the exact
time I decided publishing was for me was the time that this
novel about young girls in publishing should captivate the
public imagination. And to top it all off, I had Rona Jaffe's
autograph in a first-edition copy of her book. It was almost too
much for a girl to bear.

For three weeks of that summer of 1957 I was loaned to the
editor in chief while his secretary was on vacation. He is a
kind, mild-mannered, soft-spoken man to whom I feel I owe
a great deal. Though perched securely on Mount Olympus
himself, he made me feel that publishing was run not by gods
and goddesses but by people—people something like me. From
my vantage point at his secretary's desk I saw the feet of clay
as well as the broad shoulders of all those beautiful people.
Authors sometimes wrote junk and had to be told as much.
Editors sometimes let inaccuracies go by only to be caught up
short by book critics. Advertising decisions were sometimes
grossly off the mark.

My boss gave me manuscripts to read from the "slush" pile
of unsolicited submissions, and I believe he really read my
reader's reports. I know I have reread them dozens of times in
the past decade, marveling at the ludicrous, sophomoric critical
phrases I used with such seriousness. But I don't recall his
laughing. I *do* recall that he gave me one manuscript to read
which I reported well worth publishing. I don't know how many
editors ruled on that manuscript before it was finally published.
But several months later when I was back at college, I saw
that book listed on the New York *Times* Best Seller list and
I couldn't have been more thrilled if it were my own book.
I still feel an "insider's" sense of pride when I see reruns of
the movie version of the book on television.

I did return to college after that first summer in publishing
and I did feel a bit guilty about my Future Plans Fib. But only

because I *really* didn't want to leave that exciting job for the rigors of university life. The editor in chief somehow found time to correspond with me throughout the following academic year. I remember wanting desperately to make an indelible impression on him so that I might be allowed to return to Simon & Schuster the following summer. The fib wouldn't work a second time. I had to be employed as an up-and-up summer employee or not at all. My letters to him went something like, "I'm reading *Beowulf*. What are you publishing?" or "It's too bad there are no poets like Gerard Manley Hopkins around nowadays."

Eventually my junior year passed and I did return to Simon & Schuster for the summer of 1958. "I'll do anything," I declared to the editor in chief. And I would have willingly accepted postal-meter duty in the mail room. But somehow I ended up as secretary to the director of advertising. Here was a whole new side to publishing. I relished every single moment on that job. This advertising woman was a dynamo, a one-of-a-kind genius who truly revolutionized book advertising during her years with the firm.

I bumbled along typing her copy at fifty words per minute (with forty-five erasures), but otherwise I served her adoringly. I can still see her curled up in her big swivel chair with legs tucked under her skirt, three pencils stuck into her pony-tail hairdo and two cigarettes burning in the ashtray. I once asked her how she could always be full of fresh ideas for book after book after book. "I read them and then I care about them," she said.

In answer to my question about her own career as to how she went from secretary to director of advertising she told me a zany story that she swears is true. A psychiatrist friend of hers advised her to think positive, happy thoughts and good things would happen to her. So while she was secretary to an executive in the early days of the company, she posted on her bulletin board an index card with a word printed on it in large black letters. The word was calculated to make her think happy, positive thoughts. But the word served notice unwittingly upon her boss, who thought it was a last-ditch hint. He promoted her, gave her a substantial raise and relieved her of her secretarial chores. The word on her index card was simply: MONEY.

After graduating from college, I returned to Simon & Schuster for my "permanent" position. This time I did double duty as secretary to the director of special sales (he makes bulk sales of books to banks, airlines and other industries) and the director of mail-order advertising (he's in charge of those ads for self-help guides and beauty books which ask for coupon orders). It was again a broadening, educational employment experience—with the added bonus that by this time I had clocked enough accumulated time at the company to feel like a member of the family. I remained for almost a year and moved on only because I was still seeking a living wage. Nevertheless, it hurt to go.

For ten dollars more per week I became secretary to an editor and then secretary-assistant to the editor in chief of another publishing company, Coward-McCann. I was now an experienced editorial secretary and I remember champing at the bit. I wasn't learning and I wasn't advancing. Again, I sought out manuscript-reading assignments. But I knew that despite my bosses' sympathy for my goals, it was as a secretary that I was hired and as a secretary that I was expected to remain. By now I thought that I had cased the publishing business and decided that I wanted to be an editor. Obviously, it wasn't going to be easy. Not so obviously, it just plain wasn't going to be.

A case of acute bronchitis sent me to Cape Cod for the summer of 1960. I did free-lance reader's reports for an advertising agency specializing in book publishers' accounts. Since copywriters couldn't read every book they were assigned to write about, they worked from *précis* prepared by free lancers. This income fed me through the summer and when I returned to New York I was hired by the advertising agency as a copywriter.

And here, lo and behold, the specter of failure arose for the first time in my short but variegated working career. I was a complete and total flop. But, I mean, hopeless. For the five or six ads that I wrote which *did* end up in newspapers there were fifty which ended up in the circular file under my desk. I needed three wastebaskets at the end of each day.

Where words had come easily to me, they suddenly limped soddenly from my head to the sheet of paper where they stared back at me in their turgid splendor. About a book of Irish folk songs I wrote: "Laugh with the leprechauns at these ageless Celtic ballads" only to discover that leprechauns were tired old clichés called to duty only too often to describe any book vaguely Irish in mood or content. For a roundup ad offering one publisher's Christmas gift books I submitted the headline: "Stuff Their Stockings with Something Interesting for a Change." They stopped that one before it left the office.

After six weeks I was so uptight that I was nearly paralyzed at my desk. The director of the agency was as merciful as he was diplomatic. "You're not happy here," he said one memorable morning. With a mutual sigh of relief, I began to send out resumés to every publishing house I could think of in the hope of returning to some job where I could be a functioning human being instead of a catatonic noncopywriter.

The letter I directed to the heads of publishing houses asked for a position as a junior editor. I went to three companies for interviews for a job as a junior editor. The fourth company was Bernard Geis Associates. The job available there was for assistant director of publicity, advertising and subsidiary rights. I had done work in the subsidiary rights department for my first boss at Simon & Schuster and in the advertising department for my third and fifth bosses at Simon & Schuster. I had never done any publicity. My patron saint, father confessor and still patient boss at the ad agency strongly recommended that I take this job. Despite my freeze-up at his agency he somehow saw a spark and he felt that an energetic young publisher like Geis would ignite me again.

I was hired on the Monday before Thanksgiving 1960. I was in bad shape. My confidence was thoroughly shaken. I was entirely unfamiliar with one third of the job I was expected to do. But I had passed the milestone. I wasn't a secretary any more. Not quite a triumphant entry to the big time. But my boss and the publisher, Bernard Geis, did not know anything about my Failure. So I nursed my fears and inadequacies silently until they disappeared in the fantastic excitement of my new job.

My immediate boss was a publicity pro and a perfectionist. I learned fast. Bernard Geis is a daring publisher. So I worked on wild, unexpected books and with authors who were often celebrities first and writers second. I had my own office— six feet by nine feet—but an office with a window and a door. I took magazine writers and television producers to lunch when my boss couldn't. I booked authors on tours throughout the country. I planned publication-day parties. I was having a ball.

Six months after I was hired, Bernard Geis called me into his office. My boss was sitting there. Due to an irresistible financial offer from another publishing house, my boss would be leaving the firm. It had been decided that I would take over the three departments on a trial basis. I was told my salary. I was told the date on which I could hire my *own* assistant.

I remember muttering some inanities about being overwhelmed. Then, I made it to the ladies' room with the help of some extraterrestrial force. I don't remember blacking out, but I do remember waking up on the floor of the ladies' room, having hit my head on a sink on my way down. Hardly a propitious beginning for a young executive. But that's just the way it happened.

I suppose that was a rather melodramatic overreaction to a job offer. I had already had nine jobs. But if you realize that I was twenty-one years old, had been out of college for less than two years and had never heard of such a salary, you may begin to understand how joy can translate to shock.

That was eight years ago. I have lots to say about those eight years and all the dashing people and smashing things that have filled them. But at the beginning of this chapter I promised you that getting there was half the fun. It's also a tiny bit of sweat. I saved my own little saga for last just to prove both dicta. Oh yes, . . . about the typing . . . I have three girls working for me now. On the rare occasions when they see me typing I tap-tap along at a civilized snail's pace. But between thee and me—when nobody's looking I can type faster than two of the three of them put together. But I'll never tell. . . .

3.

Work and play

the executive way

Somehow it has come to pass. You're sitting at your well-polished desk in your sunny private office. Maybe there's a rug on the floor and your name on the door. Maybe you've been ensconced in a windowless cubicle with wall-to-wall linoleum. But it's your own office. And you know from the promotion money, the new title and the blessed privacy that you have arrived.

Executivehood comes in many shapes and sizes. It may have been a slow, sure climb with a very gradual enhancement of your position and a steady increase in your responsibilities. Or it could have happened to you, as it did to me, in one staggering jolt.

One Friday I was wedged in among the file cabinets, slaving behind a typewriter, taking messages for someone else. The next Monday I was hiring my own secretary, walking off the dimensions of my new office endless times to memorize how spacious it was, composing imaginary letters to President Kennedy, from the other end of the dictaphone for a change, and pinching myself to be absolutely sure I was me.

Welcome to the first timers club

Whatever your experience turns out to be, there will un-
questionably come a moment in the Great Transition when
you realize that you are a virgin big shot. There has to be
a first time for *everything*. And if you've never taken the vows
of executivehood you may be amazed at the number of firsts
that Mother—and even your most well-meaning mentors—never
told you about. For every thrilling, satisfying first, there will be
another one that shatters your ego and reddens your cheeks.
You may long for the good old days of secretarial immunity.
You may yearn for the sanctuary of the electric typewriter
where to err is human; to erase is fine.

The size of your problems and the enormity of your mistakes
are apt to grow with the stature of your job. An eraser is an
impotent weapon when the crises involve elite people rather
than an elite typeface.

There's an old axiom, "Girls who run around in circles seldom
become big wheels." They merely become dizzy dames. How
are you going to stay loose? How are you going to cultivate
your three "Cs," competence, confidence and cool?

The best mental exercise for nubile executive jitters is borrowed from a course I once took at the maternity clinic. To
soothe the formless fears of a group of young mothers-to-be our
instructor counseled us to look searchingly at every woman
who passed us in the street. "They won't appear especially
valorous or heroic or martyred," the instructor guaranteed. "But
nearly every woman you'll see who is wearing a wedding ring
has been through childbirth. If they *all* can do it, so can you."

Not very profound advice by any measure. But it did the
job for all the slightly panicked pregnant girls in the class.

It was a cosmic truth worth pondering: we were each having a baby for the first time, but it wasn't the first time that a baby was ever born.

When you give birth to a new you in a new, important role, you would do well to remember that you're not the first little girl to move into the big time. Tadpoles undergo a metamorphosis into frogs. Secretaries and clerks can change into lovely lady executives with one flick of somebody's magic wand. Fulfilling the demands of the new role may be embarrassing, painful and utterly baffling. But if you are superconsciously aware that every executive you ever admired had to go through the same Great Transition that now faces you—you will calm those jitters in a jiffy.

I don't know of any top-level lady who claims to have done *everything* right the first time around. Even with a carefully equipped Survival Kit no one is indemnified against all the ghastly gaffs and frightful *faux pas* in the book. That's only because the book on Virgin Executive's Most Embarrassing Moments hasn't been written yet. And if it were, it would be out of date before the first copy was off press.

What's your "image?"

You'll have to find your own personal style at the same time that you learn all the basics. You'll have to make your own unique little mistakes. You may want to do some revamping of your image—an overused word but as serviceable a one as any to describe the external picture you project. More people will be watching you do more meaningful things. You will be representing more than just yourself. You will, in a real sense, be embodying the job you perform and representing the company that has chosen to make you a special somebody. How special you are going to be is entirely up to you.

In the novel *Breakfast at Tiffany's,* Holly Golightly's closest friends decided that she was not just a kook or a phony. Holly was a *real* phony. There is such a breed in business too. No girl was born knowing how to negotiate for a million-dollar parcel of real estate with perfect aplomb. Breaking up with a long-time beau comes a lot easier to a woman than breaking the news to an ad agency that it is about to be stripped of five hundred thousand dollars' worth of billings. It takes a lot of guts and a little bit of phoniness to charm an oil millionaire into investing money in your client's three-act play about civil rights.

Grooming yourself privately but conscientiously for the role of real phony shouldn't make you squirm. The word "real" is as operative as the word "phony." If everyone was completely honest, we could be regaled with stories of *necessary* phoniness from any passing executive. Or from anyone who moves in a civilized, social context, for that matter. What, after all, is good manners or etiquette if not "necessary phoniness?" Just imagine the chaos and the maelstrom of hurt feelings if all of us went around being ourselves.

"I have a splitting headache," the comptroller might say. "I'll sign your salary check some other time."

"Don't kid me," the fashion editor might say to the dress designer. "You've created the boyish look because you're a woman-hating homosexual."

No, it would never do. And it doesn't. So why not start early in your executivehood determining what elements of your personality are vital expressions of your real self—and not to be tampered with for any reason—and what are the layers or portions of you that are malleable and available to adjustment? Don't mess around with your values. Leave your ethics intact.

Scrutinize your job commitment and be sure you're sure where aggressiveness ends and consideration for others begins.

Once you have drawn the boundaries at the untouchable truth of your personality, you can concentrate on style with a clear conscience. Anticipating executive growing pains and preparing the means, methods and manner of handling each hurdle is perfectly kosher. Why not look good, first shot out of the box? Why be a mindlessly honest schnook who blunders through life's little tough spots? There are the doers and the done-tos. The done-tos are more often than not done in by their own "honest" reactions to everything. It's sensible, not cynical, to censor yourself smoothly and gracefully.

Leave the love beads at home

Starting with a simple concept and a universally accepted one, we can best define executive preparedness in terms of a physical reappraisal. I used to be bugged about my essential honesty, too. As a business-world beginner, I was a Greenwich Village girl from top to toe. I was antimake-up, prosandals and more apt to be swathed in a burlap poncho than in a Kimberly knit. Where other secretaries wore a string of pearls and gold button earrings, I could be found with a rope of painted apple-seed beads around my neck and three Persian fertility rings on the fingers of one hand. My hair was three feet long—and never had those locks been raped by hair spray, rollers or rats. (And that was in the heyday of curly artichoke style and the rigid sculpture of the beehive!)

My appearance must have presented the instant challenge: take it or leave it. My zealously "honest" image was actually a dishonest flaunting of convention. Bohemianism is fine on Macdougal Street. But four dozen blocks uptown it's a real question whether the image in a less colorful setting doesn't become a caricature of itself. The "look" didn't weather the subway ride. But it took me several years to shed it without feeling like a middle-class sellout. I was a dutiful, hard-working secretary waiting to be discovered and promoted for my *true* self. Then one morning my boss said: "I'd love to send you over to the sales conference at the Plaza Hotel, but you look like a refugee from Brooks Costume shop."

He was smiling. It was a joshing comment which our comfortable relationship allowed him to make with impunity. But suddenly I saw what he saw when he looked at me. I was as carefully dressed as the next gal, but my boss couldn't be blamed for not seeing past the beatnik accouterments. He was a man raised on four-in-hand neckties and tuned in to women with straight seams in their stockings and tortoise-shell combs in their hair. To him I was lovable, kooky but absolutely *not* the ideal outside representative of a publishing house.

Does it sound ridiculous to say that I searched my soul? Even so, it felt like an apocalyptic self-analysis. Could I dress up to Madison Avenue standards without betraying my own? You're damned straight I could. And I did—with very little concession to phoniness. It seemed that only a light-pink lipstick, a french-knot chignon and a half-dozen pair of high-heel shoes provided my entree into respectability.

I didn't land an executive job as soon as I revised my wardrobe. But there was a discernible difference in the way coworkers approached me. My boss took me out for a few fancy lunches. Most of all, I no longer thought of myself as a kid on leave from Greenwich Village posturing for a few hours in the adult world. Sometimes transformations come from the outside and work in. For me, it happened that way. In my grown-up clothes I was treated like a woman and so I learned that *effect* has *affect*.

From the metamorphosis of clothing and make-up, it was a short step to reason how other adjustments—other acts of necessary phoniness—might in the long run serve the *real* me better than the real me ever could.

Lunchtime: food, drink and fun and games

As a female in a predominantly male preserve you will quickly see how these personality adjustments take on unique shadings. You will not only operate on the levels of executive-to-executive or executive-to-subordinate but on the age-old bed of nails involving the confrontation of the sexes. Here is where behavioral amenities really pay off.

Take the lunch date, for example. Your first time away from Nedick's or the corner luncheonette may be exciting in and of itself. But if you get too carried away by the elegant décor of a fancy luncheon spa or the gastronomical delicacies and astronomical prices on the menu, you may neglect the niceties. No matter how high-powered you've suddenly become, you're still the little lady and he's still the big man. Everyone takes it for granted that a woman who picks up the tab for a business lunch is doing so with company money. The man's ego allows for that. Sexual role-playing is temporarily suspended when you're armed with petty cash or a credit card or a restaurant house account in the firm's name. Nevertheless, a certain façade should be maintained. Your method matters more than the reality of money matters. Because lunch dates can establish a personal intimacy and a bond of friendship that enhances all your business dealings with an individual, it would be unforgivable to wound his ego on a technicality.

Here is the lunch-date lesson that I learned well after garnering the advice of every girl I knew who had graduated from the hamburgers with ketchup and relish to chopped sirloin of beef with sauce Béarnaise:

You may invite him to lunch. But you ask him to suggest the restaurant.

You may offer to make the reservation in your name. But if he has recommended his favorite noontime haunt he should be permitted to make the reservation even though it's understood that you're going to pay the bill.

When the date of the lunch has been agreed in advance between you and the man, and only time and place remain to be settled, it's customary to put the proceedings into the hands of your two secretaries. Instruct your secretary to suggest both time and place and to offer to make the reservation in your name. But she too should defer if his secretary communicates that *his* choice is something different on either count.

If you arrive at the table first, don't order a drink while you're waiting for him. When he gets there he may feel compelled to order one just to keep you company, even if he's off the sauce. Or if he resists and doesn't join you in a cocktail, what will he do with himself while you finish your solitary sipping? It's best to wait until he arrives and let the suggestion of cocktails be his to make or not.

Which brings up the crucial point that ordering food, drink or dancing girls is *always* done by the man. I don't care if the captain is your uncle and the waiter lives next door to you. You shouldn't give your order to either of them under any circumstances—unless, perhaps, your luncheon companion has laryngitis, which is unlikely if you're there to *talk* business. The man requests the menus, asks you for your choice of appetizer and entrée, signals for the captain or waiter and gives both your order and his own. In the middle of the meal, should you need more butter or a glass of water tell your companion and let him worry about catching the waiter's eye. Nothing is more

appalling than the sound of a woman's shrill voice sum-
moning the captain to request a steak knife or complain
about lukewarm coffee while the man at her side is numb,
mute and helpless. You can pay his bill but you must let
him forage for the food and fight the battles. It's been
that way for centuries.

The moment of truth: how does a girl gracefully pay the
check? There are two easy ways that have always worked
for me. If we are at my favorite restaurant where I am
known by the maître d' or one of the captains and where
I am able to make certain arrangements in advance then
I use Plan A: I signal to the captain with an imperceptible
nod to indicate when I want the check. It is brought to
me with a voucher already filled out with the details of
my house account and requiring only my signature. I just
sign it and it is whisked away again with nary a pause
in the conversation. At the end of each month when the
bills come in, I add the gratuities and check the addition
from the privacy of my own office. At a less familiar
restaurant, Plan B goes into effect: When I'm ready to
leave, if my companion hasn't already requested the check,
I ask him to call for it while at the same time tossing
off one of a great many possible face-saver remarks to
re-establish that I am not *personally* paying for him. I might
say, "Bernard Geis Associates just sold a book to the movies.
We're flush. It's my treat this time." Or, if the comment
happily applies, I might boast, "*The Exhibitionist* has been
on the best-seller lists twenty weeks today so Bernard
Geis Associates is feeling especially munificent. This one's
on us." If my businessman friend really insists—such as
saying at least *twice* that he'll pay—I give in gracefully.

Once it's clear that you are the one who is settling accounts
you can still be incurably feminine *and* sensible at the
same time. Whether using cash or a credit card, you'll have
to grapple with the higher mathematics of the tip. You
needn't do long division on your napkin. Ask your companion to figure out the tip for you. A man does that sort

of thing so often that it's instinct with him. Your request also returns to him some portion of the male function. (And if you think that makes it a phony ploy, you're just being silly. In this situation I would rather *be* calculating than *do* the calculating.)

Your last stop may be the check room. If your coat has been checked, give the claim stub to your companion. He gets your coat and tips the attendant. *Never* fight him on that petty expenditure.

Those are the rules of the lunch game as I see them. Obviously, they are only superficial how-tos. But if you master them, your first few lunch dates will not be fraught with *faux pas* which can only complicate your already burdensome new role. Your major concern, of course, is the deal you want to discuss, the overall impression you wish to create, the friendship you hope to establish. As a brand-new executive taking on unfamiliar responsibilities, your first lunch date with a client or an important contact will set the tone for all your future dealings. You can make or break a business relationship as you make a toast or break bread with a man. The social setting that a restaurant—as opposed to an office—provides can get you off to a good head start. If you are sensitive to the refinements of male/female business etiquette you've taken another step in the right direction. The eight tips outlined above will become second nature to you before you've even chalked up eight business lunches, I guarantee. But if you are as efficient and as cautious as a friend of mine is, then consider a trial run. This girl took her boy friend to a fancy restaurant for a "let's pretend" business lunch at which she tested herself and asked the guy's candid comments and reactions. (For a ten- or fifteen-dollar investment you can enlist the services of a platonic pal, beau or relative for the same purpose.)

The younger you are at the point when you ascend to full executivehood, the more comfortable you will feel about turning over to your male business companion all the traditional masculine responsibilities at the restaurant. Youth as well as femininity may dictate a certain respectful reticence. Later on, as your confidence increases and your personal style is refined, you may want to assert your ideas of feminine equality. By all means, be true to your instincts. If you've grown fond of two or three local restaurants, suggest them. If you feel right about ordering for yourself and the man or paying the check or dealing with the captain, forge ahead. You may spearhead a new wave of reform to clear the way for other ladies who feel that role-playing in restaurants is ridiculous.

Playing it by ear

Beyond those decisions about luncheon etiquette you'll have to be on your own. Too many varying factors come into play for anyone to generalize about—the pun is irresistible—the meat-and-potatoes substance of the lunch date. This is where you'll make a pitch or make a judgment. This is where you'll woo his business and win his friendship. This is where you'll talk about *your* summer vacation and *his* son's problems with the draft. This is where he'll decide just how knowledgeable you are despite your age, sex and beauty.

Wouldn't it be great if you could feed into some mammoth computer the name of your lunch partner and receive back in forty-two seconds a full dossier on him? You might find out that he is president of the local Humane Society in time to leave your leopard-skin coat in the closet and show up in the gray tweed. You'd know in advance that he deplores women in hanging earrings or that he would rather talk about metaphysical poetry than explain to you his magazine's editorial policies. And while you are about it, you might check ahead of time whether he is married, divorced, single, queer or straight.

Lacking such a miracle machine you have to feel your way—and it's just as well that you don't know all his hang-ups. Both of you start out together *tabula rasa:* clean slate. You write your impressions as you go, he writes his. If he wants to plunge right in selling his promotional wares, let him. If he spreads his color brochures all over the celery and olives, you'll just have to forego the finger foods and focus on his sales spiel. If he comes on suspicious of your credentials, let him put you through your paces. You're a woman and you've been promoted to the executive level and it wasn't because you slept with your boss. It was because you could handle the job. Surely you can handle any lunch-table third degree that some pompous doubting Thomas throws your way.

Don't be alarmed if you don't get around to talking a syllable about business at your business lunches. Unless you're in a very square, button-down firm, nobody really expects you to come back with an order for ten thousand units or a signed check in your purse after two hours at P. J. Clarke's. Your boss expects you to make *contact*. He hopes that you'll be enchanting and intelligent and that you'll make a friend for the company. If you make a deal over the demitasse, so much the better. But if you don't, there's always the telephone call, the office meeting or the official letter at your disposal to tie up the loose ends of a commitment once a luncheon companion becomes a convert.

Usually—though not always—I get around to describing the books on my company's publishing schedule before the end of a lunch date. It comes up without fanfare or announcement. When one of our forthcoming books was about the stock market and I was lunching with a television producer I knew to be a big speculator, it was natural to mention a few advance tips that I remembered from reading the manuscript. From there we covered the remainder of the publishing list and the availability of several authors for the man's talk show. If Bernard Geis Associates books had never been mentioned it would still have been an enjoyable and extremely profitable lunch. He told me his plans for future program subjects (several of which I noted would provide perfect vheicles for my authors); he let it be known that he resented anyone working with his show via his assistant and he confided that he was going into motion-picture production (and wouldn't I be in on the ground floor when it came time to submit book properties for consideration). We finished up by trading Polish, Irish, Italian and Jewish jokes. Exit laughing. The perfect business lunch.

Some of my favorite business-lunch companions are the lady editor of a paperback house with whom I can talk endlessly about natural childbirth; the correspondent of a London newspaper who is a mine of information about U.S. foreign policy; the tough-talking, hard-drinking columnist whose anecdotes about athletes, bookies, congressmen and cowboys supply me with enough cocktail-party conversation for a month of Saturday nights; the press agent who knows Broadway characters like I know my own family; the food editor who can make me drool about great gourmet meals he has known even while I'm in the midst of an epicurean delight on my own plate (*and* he gives me recipes); the movie agent who can make skiing sound more fascinating than sex; the widowed advertising man who endearingly asks my advice about his romances.

These are the kind of people to whom you devote the *real* you as well as the most honorable, straightforward business you. Remember a man's war record, if he ever told it to you. Ask about his new grandchildren, the property he bought in

Vermont or the whiplash injury he complained about last time you met. Listen to business coups that may have nothing to do with you. Giving in to friendship will never prevent you from striking a shrewd bargain when you have to. Let yourself like the man or woman sitting across the table and you'll let yourself in for a lot more than just a good lunch.

Hail the long-suffering secretary

Some weeks you'll go out to long lunches five days out of five and some weeks will go by without so much as a fingerprint on your Diners' Club card. The backlog of paperwork on your desk or interdepartmental meetings or spring shopping expeditions may determine how often you hit the glamourous luncheon oases. You exercise some control over whom you have lunch with and how often. But whether or not you want it, one relationship persists at close range five days out of five, through sleet and hail, through headaches and happy moods, on great days and on grim ones. Your secretary and you will develop a symbiotic relationship which defies comparison to any other human contact. Forget everything we've said about *being* a secretary. Once you *have* a secretary, different rules go into effect and it's a new ball game.

In eight years of executivehood I have had four secretaries. One left to have a baby and retire (she has since asked to come back part-time); one left to get married and retire (she *has* come back to pitch in during busy periods); one was fired by me on grounds of incompatibility, and one has been with me for over six years. That's a pretty sensational record, I think.

Two of my secretaries were older than I. Three of the four have become personal friends. My present secretary has, in the years we've worked together, loaned and borrowed clothes, attended my wedding, baby-sat for my children, taken the rap for dozens of my mistakes and exhibited the kind of total loyalty that went out of style with duels at dawn. She is a raving beauty—high cheekbones, great eyes, size six figure, the works. She has typed forty form letters in one morning, transcribed two dictation tapes in the afternoon and emerged fresh and pleasant for an evening of checking in guests at an author's cocktail party. Ask her the name of the company that donated liquor for our Harpo Marx publication-date party six years ago and you can lay bets that she'll remember company, contact's name and the labels on the bottles.

The best I could do for you when you first need a secretary would be to send Judy over for a month or so. Failing that, perhaps some fundamental dos and don'ts will help you keep head above water until you find a Judy of your own.

Don't forget what it felt like when you were a secretary, armed with the classified ads and a sturdy pair of walking shoes. You wanted the truth about the job being offered. You hoped for a clue to the boss's personality. You wanted a hint about where the job might lead. When you are interviewing applicants, *don't* play female games of one-upmanship. *Don't* ask embarrassing and unnecessary questions (do you really have to know why she got divorced?) and *don't* focus on her physical statistics. (I never understood what height and weight had to do with a secretarial job anyway.) If there's a chance that she might travel to the branch offices or become your assistant if the department expands as you hope, tell her. And by the same token, if the vacation policy is cruel and inhuman—like compulsory one-week vacations which coincide with the four-day national Fourth of July weekend—or if her desk is right next to the mimeograph machine, tell her that too. This is the time and the place for empathy. What you wanted when you were job hunting, if you can resurrect those feelings, provides a safe guide to what your applicants are seeking as well.

Do tell her, once you've hired her, that she's your very first secretary ever. Assuming you've screened carefully and chosen well, she will probably be a sweet young thing willing to sweat out your growing pains with you—if you're honest with her. It's absurd to play big-deal executive with the one person who is close enough to you to find out otherwise. *Do* make her an ally. Trust her with your professional fears. Your professional expertise will not be in question. You can keep your distance or mark the status differential, if you like, with personal formalities. If she's an old-hand secretary she can help you become an executive by showing you what you should expect of her—and yourself.

A friend of mine did exactly that. She hired a mature lady who had chalked up fifteen years of secretarial experience. My friend was the pro about book publicity and fortunately her confidence in her ability prevented the secretary from completely assuming a motherly role. Nevertheless, this older woman relished the role of tutor. She taught my friend how to use a dictaphone, how to use a secretary for interception of phone calls and visitors, what to demand in terms of work output and how to best organize her files. This particular friend had not ever been a secretary herself, so she was even at a loss when it came to such basics as proper letter format and the wonders of a desk appointment calendar. She needed more than a symbiotic give-and-take. But the secretary didn't mind that the relationship was primarily a one-way street with the boss getting the best of the bargain.

Do keep an eye on her roving eye. If she's looking with hungry glances at a job opening in another department, *don't* feel betrayed. Should she show signs of coveting your job, don't be shocked. After all, making it was your aim too.

Your secretary may just be working for the money. Maybe she's supplementing her husband's modest income or socking it away for a trip around the world. She could be one of those unmotivated ladies who wants no more than job security and a decent paycheck. Whichever category fits is not at issue. I'm only suggesting that you figure out which type of girl she is and anticipate how her aspirations are likely to affect you.

If you value her and it's money she wants, get her a raise in the most reasonable amount of time you can manage. If you value her and you sense that she's starting to get the itch for moving onward and upward, have an honest talk. Will she be content if you add to her duties some function that may be more stimulating? Does she want a different title than secretary? Is she hell-bent on finding a more responsible job? If the latter is the case, then you'll be doing both of you a favor if you let her go with a superspecial recommendation. Let her off the hook before she begins to resent that her fealty to you is standing in the way of her self-improvement.

Don't perpetuate the little acts of discrimination that plagued you. Men in this man's world are doing enough to keep married women and working mothers from competing equally for white-collar jobs. *Don't* be a Benedict Alice when it's your turn to hire a secretary. Married women don't require that many allowances or privileges. *They'll* worry about accommodating their other life to the demands of the job. *You* don't have to.

As I said before, qualifications count, personal statistics don't. One of these days aren't you going to get married and have children? And don't you think you might want to remain a working executive? How will you react if some company turns *you* away because of your marital or motherly duties?

Despite the main premise of this book, I suppose that it is fortunate that *some* girls like being secretaries and truly have no further ambition. Like Judy, my own gem of a right-hand maiden, some secretaries like the excitement of working with and for an executive whose area of responsibility is fun and interesting, but they loathe the idea of carrying the ball alone. I give Judy all the autonomy she can stomach. She's the one who calls a halt if I've unloaded too many decision-making assignments onto her desk and into her lap. I've learned her fortes and her phobias as well as she has learned mine. I know that on the telephone she can handle the knottiest problem with exceptional diplomacy. But ask her to do the same dirty work in person—i.e., turning down the lecture requests for authors or dealing with advertising space salesmen—and she freezes. She'll take on a miserably complicated project involving clearance of dozens of copyrighted photographs but she breaks out into hives if I request that she attend a publicity seminar and report on it in a memo. She'll suggest a great design approach for a mailing piece but she pales at the idea of negotiating prices for it with the printer.

The secretary-boss relationship is the closest thing to a marriage. (Surely that accounts for the apprehension that wives of male executives feel about their husbands' hirelings.) When the executive is also a woman, the plot thickens. Perhaps the secretary-boss relationship then resembles something more akin to a roommate situation or a mother-daughter association. Whatever the simile, the intimacy is clearly determined by hours spent together. Finding the exactly right stance between friendliness and formality is the key to an effective working arrangement.

As a brand-new executive you will be guided largely by three factors beyond your control: your own age, the age of your secretary and the basic atmosphere of your office. No matter how irrelevant comparative ages may be to business functions, a forty-year-old secretary working for a twenty-five-year-old boss is going to have age on her mind, whereas with the ages and positions reversed neither party gives it a thought. Do you absolutely refuse to hire a secretary who is more than four or five years your senior? No, not unless you're the kind of girl who gives up in *anticipation* of difficulties. The sensible thing is to face the age factor head on and immediately. If you are impressed with an applicant's experience, qualifications and personal manner in an interview, why not ask her point-blank how she would feel about taking orders from a "youngster" such as yourself. Her answer will force her to put feelings into words. You should be able to judge by her forthrightness, by how she reacts to the question having been posed so directly, as well as by what she claims will be the case.

"I notice on your resumé that you have a daughter in college," you might comment. "Does it affect your attitude toward me to realize that I am just a few years older than your own daughter?"

Your applicant may be amused at the question. She may ponder it seriously. She may turn defensive. Whatever she does she won't be able to mask her real feelings entirely. And if there are warning signs to be interpreted, they will be waving like a red flag at the interview, giving you ample chance for a getaway.

One nubile lady boss asked a similar question and got a red-flag answer if I ever heard one:

"Now, don't you worry, dearie," her fiftyish applicant soothed. "My daughter and I get on just fine together and I'm sure you and I can too."

If the "dearie" didn't flash the warning signal, the maternal tone of voice *did*.

On the other side of the coin is the secretary who is so clearly a contemporary that familiarity threatens to undermine the delicate working balance. Just because you both graduated from college in the class of '62, you both wear signature scarves and body shirts and you both subscribe to *The New Yorker* doesn't mean that you need allow complete equality to upset your equilibrium. Someone has to give the orders and someone has to carry them out and the plain fact is that she works for you. Despite the external similarities—and even if you suspect that you and your secretary are equals through and through— you're the one with the experience and the know-how. Knowledge is power, and power, exercised judiciously and sensitively, will keep the status lines as well defined as you feel they need be. (Strange as it may sound, I think you'll find that the longer you work in an executive capacity the less you'll care about this role-playing anyway. When you take it for granted that your secretary and you are a team and you are captain, that's when you'll both be winners.)

I know of one case where familiarity breeds constant complications. A girl I'll call Hannah has made her secretary both a pet and a pal. The secretary knows as much about Hannah as Hannah's analyst does. Hannah has taken the girl with her to parties having nothing to do with their business life. They go to the movies together when neither has a date. The secretary has seen Hannah fall to pieces over a love affair. Hannah has mediated disputes between the secretary and her boy friend. The secretary was in on the trauma and the travel plans when Hannah went to Puerto Rico for an abortion.

This might sound like a cozy setup with friend and confidante only an intercom buzz away. But a peculiar state of affairs exists now where Hannah simply cannot feel comfortable about asking the secretary to do routine chores. Without meaning to be an opportunist, the secretary takes advantage of Hannah's permissiveness. Hannah ends up typing many of her own letters rather than overburdening the girl. Hannah stays late to file correspondence. She can't bring herself to criticize the secretary for sloppy typing or for monopolizing the telephone lines with personal phone calls. You might say that Hannah gained a friend and lost a secretary.

Suppose now that you were Hannah. Realizing your mistake you recognize that you cannot undo the intimacies or withdraw the rapport. You decide that you must fire her.

The fine art of firing

How to fire without leaving third-degree burns is an art in itself. I have fired one of my secretaries and two of my assistants. In all three cases I was unable to practice the advice of a brilliant advertising woman who claims that the best way to get rid of someone is to find him or her a better job. If you can in good conscience recommend your misfit secretary or inept assistant to some other company or department, then by all means give her a helping hand rather than just a shove out the door. You don't want to hurt her or punish her. You just want to replace her.

If no such opportunity presents itself or if you can't bring yourself to unload your personnel problem on a friend, then gird your loins or loosen your girdle—whichever will best prepare you for your next first: discharging an employee.

The first time I fired an assistant I did everything wrong. I took her out to lunch to do it. I opened the subject as soon as we sat down at the table. By the main course I had had my say but I was trapped for another hour at least. I was stupid enough to feel that I had to catalogue her faults. "You've been late four days out of every five for the past three months," I chanted. "You have consistently shown poor judgment in booking important authors on unimportant radio shows on ten-kilowatt stations while ignoring major television producers whom you happen to dislike. You have betrayed private office con-

fidences about one author to another. You have taken school
chums of yours to lunch and charged it on your expense account."

It's not too surprising, now that I look back on it, to report
that she reacted first with the retaliatory tactics of a street
fighter. She denied my accusations. She defended her behavior.
She bombarded me with criticisms of her own. When these
tactics only served to toughen me further, she broke down and
cried and begged for another chance.

The whole experience was so ghastly and painful that I dread
thinking of it even now. I ended up so ashamed of my heart-
lessness that I lavished apologies upon her and canceled the
whole discharge by the time we were on coffee and dessert.
Her second chance lasted about two months more. Naturally,
the same faults cropped up eventually and I had to lower the
boom once again. This time I was a veteran of trial by firing.
I told her that the budget for my department had been cut and I
had to let her go. That excuse and three weeks' severance pay
spared us both a repetition of a lunch that only a sado-masochist
would want to experience twice.

The next assistant that I had to fire probably believes to this
day that she did us a favor by leaving. She was a congenital
liar, starting with her claim that she had graduated from college. (I had already hired her by the time that the school
answered my request for a reference with the formal statement: "Miss N. is not and has never been a student at this
university.") During her six months on the job I received dis-
turbing reports that she had represented herself as the publisher's wife, offering publishing contracts and wild-money
promises to all sorts of oddballs and semicelebrities whom she
had wanted to impress in her travels. Finally, I gave Miss N.
two thoroughly palatable reasons why I had decided that *she*
should leave: I was finding it difficult to work comfortably with

someone older than myself (which she was), and I felt she was
too good for the job (which she wasn't) and should seek a
more responsible position either in publishing or in the theatre
where her greatest interest lay. Miss N. was very suggestible.
She left us with hugs and kisses and fond farewells. And guess
what? It turns out I was more right than I knew. She is now a
moderately successful actress and scriptwriter in Hollywood,
where everything is bigger than life including the fibs.

My third and last firing was mercifully uneventful. I had
learned my lesson well. Not a word about this secretary's
myriad shortcomings passed my lips. I said nothing about her
impossible slowness or her incredibly simple-minded errors—
she was the sort who would file all correspondence under "L"
for "letters" if you didn't stop her in time. I couldn't properly
fib that budget cuts required me to live without a secretary.
I *was* concerned about the girl's feelings because she was
inordinately shy and sensitive. This very realization was my
keynote. I was able to use the truth to fire her for her own
good as well as for mine.

"You seem to be nervous lately, Catherine," I said one day
after hours.

"Well, yes, I do feel under terrible pressure what with all the
deadlines and rush jobs," she said.

"I'm sorry to say that you've just described the life force of
any publicity department. The deadlines and rush jobs are what
keep things ticking. What worries me is that we're ticking
away too fast for your internal clock," I ventured.

"Huh?" she said.

"What I mean is, Catherine, you may not be temperamentally
suited to the pace of this work. You seem so placid and calm.
Maybe you would be happier in a less hectic working atmosphere."

"Yes, I probably could get a lot more done if things didn't

happen all the time before I've finished with other things," she said.

"Exactly what I meant," I sighed. Now we were getting somewhere. "Do you think you might like working for a textbook publisher or a library or maybe a rare book dealer?"

"Oh, I don't really have to stay in publishing. Just any old typing job that I could relax in. That's what I really need." She had opened the door wide. I helped her out gently.

"I'll gladly give you a fine reference as soon as you can find exactly the job that suits you. Take whatever time you need to go out on interviews or to employment agencies," I said. And she did go job hunting on company time and in two days she found what she wanted and in two weeks she was gone.

Don't put yourself or your employee on the hot seat when you have to fire her. Let her off easy and let her out with her dignity. Some boss somewhere will find your reject the answer to his secretarial prayers. Incompatibility rather than clear-cut faults or shortcomings accounts for most firings. I think that the trick is to fire without raking up the coals.

Full credit to the credit card

No executive firsts can quite compare to the Lunch Date, the Secretary and Firing Procedures for sheer melodrama and for the varieties of potential disaster. But I have a special place in my heart for the credit card—an executive's badge of freedom. The credit card is hard to get but easy to use. If your company gives you one you'll feel a serene confidence wash over you the minute you sign your indelible name in the proper space and tuck it into your wallet. Never again need you be shackled to your cash reserves. Last-minute ad-

dition of three guys at the dinner table? You needn't finger
your dollar bills under the tablecloth to be sure you can absorb
the guests. Sudden impulse to send flowers to a salesman's wife
in the maternity ward? Charge it. A credit card is a status
symbol to some people. To me it is a necessary crutch without
which I would have fallen on my face countless times.

As we all know, you can charge anything from air fare to
kangaroo meat on the various credit plans. I have used my cards
for all the standard executive indulgences: meals, limousines,
planes, trains, flowers and fruit baskets. But the time I remember
bowing in reverence in the direction of the Diners' Club offices
was the night I used my card for Brendan Behan. Brendan was
best known for his book *Borstal Boy*, for his plays *The Hostage*
and *The Quare Fellow,* and for his bottomless mug.

The boisterous, unpredictable Irishman had been in my care
for the three days since he had arrived unannounced from
Dublin. When I say "in my care," I mean I was assigned to him
full time to keep him happy, off booze and at the typewriter.
A manuscript we had under contract was seriously overdue.
Brendan had obliged us very nicely for the first three days. He
was writing at a typewriter we had rented for him. He was on
the wagon and he was positively blooming in a New York City
which seemed to love him as much as it laughed at him.

On this one night I was to meet Brendan at the Chelsea
Hotel and escort him to one of the television studios where he
was to be the featured guest on a late-night show. When I
arrived, Brendan was not in his room. He was not in the lobby
nor was he singing Irish songs in the hallways of the hotel as he'd
been known to do. He wasn't visiting modern dancer Katherine
Dunham or playwright Arthur Miller or other inhabitants of the
hotel. Finally, I got the word from a derelict on the street outside (the men of the street were as dear to Brendan as Arthur

Miller was) that Brendan was in the Silver Rail Bar and he was very definitely *off* the wagon.

So far off he was that I couldn't find him when I walked into the tavern. He had passed out on the floor under a rear table.

His clothes were filthy. He was covered by an unsightly layer of sawdust, which had stuck to his liquor-stained trousers. He was a mess but he was—as always—salvageable. I knelt down to stir him back to life.

"Letty, me love," he said from his prone position, "what in St. Peter's name are you doin' down here on the barroom floor?"

I reminded him of the television show.

"For Jasus' sake, we've got a lifetime to make it up there," he twinkled, raising his barrel-shaped bulk up onto a chair. "Have yourself a bit of the gargle while I get me affairs in order."

The brogue was thicker than usual. I was ready to call the studio and cancel his appearance but Brendan wouldn't hear of it. He was not a man to disappoint his audience. He toddled off to the men's room, returning a few minutes later with a well-scrubbed face and the old impish look in his eyes. I began to hope that we might go through with the evening after all. But his clothing was in a hopeless condition. And it was the only set of clothes he had with him in America—having left Dublin on the spur of the moment, as it were.

If he were being interviewed on radio, naturally it wouldn't have concerned me. But with millions of viewers tuning in on television I simply couldn't abide the thought of Brendan Behan exposing his most disheveled self to the multitudes. He was the *enfant terrible* of the American theatre. He was a "character." But he was a lovable, angelic man and I wasn't going to allow him to play the shoddy clown.

It was past nine o'clock. All the department stores and shops were closed. *Nobody* I knew could possibly donate a presentable suit of clothes that would fit Brendan's Teddy-bear shape.

Inspiration struck. My Diners' Club directory booklet listed two men's haberdashery shops in the Broadway area. Maybe, just maybe, the Times Square location would indicate a later closing time. We took a cab uptown. The first store was brightly lit and open for business. In record time Brendan Behan was fitted into a conservative blue suit, a blue shirt (for television), a new tie and a belt (his old trousers were held up with a cord). He absolutely refused to buy a set of underwear, protesting: "Me and Marilyn Monroe, we never wear the stuff." He also insisted on keeping his old shoes, though he allowed us to press on him a pair of socks.

And so it was that Brendan arrived at the television studio in great sartorial splendor and, though still a bit soused, he carried off a spectacularly memorable interview.

As for me and my credit card, Brendan had nothing but the highest gratitude. "Letty, me love," he said when it was all over, "may all yer sons be bishops!"

4.

The
other woman

*I*n the best of all possible worlds, bright, energetic women would be recognized, rewarded, encouraged and afforded every possible opportunity for advancement. They would rise gracefully to the level of their capacities. Industry would absorb them without the earth quaking. Men would accept them as colleagues without the accompaniment of celestial fireworks. Would that this were the case.

But we all know that the earth does tremble and firecrackers do explode whenever a female breaks through to the executive ranks. It used to be even worse than it is today. Perhaps that explains why so many women now in top positions are tough, hard-driving powerhouses. These women had to scratch and claw to get where they are. No one was pleading their cause before the Commission for Human Rights fifteen or twenty years ago. They made it the hard way—all alone—and fighting every step of the route. In many cases, these women live up to the stereotypes. And it may take another ten years for the new breed of female executive to replace the old toughies.

There is room for us all, without the scratching and the clawing. But you may encounter enough specimens of the old breed of fighting tigress to merit a word or two of warning.

Hordes of other women have the same idea you do—and

not all of them are as nice as you. While attempting to penetrate
the hallowed inner sanctum of the man's world—and even
once you're inside—you are going to run into and over other
girls, ladies, women with seniority, casting-couch sexperts, female
computers and bitches-on-wheels who constitute the endless
stumbling blocks that make the journey so hazardous.

If you've been innocently scampering and cavorting in those
halcyon fields where women are girl friends and confidantes
and bosom, blood buddies, then you'd better tune in carefully.
The other woman in your business life may not be aware of
our precept that there's room for all of us at the top. Unless a
gal is a pal since play-pen days or a very close and dear first
cousin, you'd be well advised to insure yourself against betrayal
with Lloyd's of London. It's a high-risk area.

A princess among the witches

Very occasionally one encounters that rare princess who realizes that your success is really no skin off her nose. Most likely
this woman will become your best friend or your most trusted
and adored mentor. You may warm to her on first meeting. Or
she may grow slowly, but surely, to be a friend.

If she's a contemporary colleague, play it straight with her.
Be a friend first, a girl-on-the-go second. If you're genuinely
happy at her successes and if she breaks out the champagne
for your little plateaus, then hang out the moon. *Quelle* feat!
Friends that can truly share your victories are hard to find. The
ones that seem solicitous and sorrowful and understanding when
you're miserable are a dime a dozen. Misery *does* love company
—but joy often stands alone. So if you've got a girl friend who
is with you all the way, treasure her.

If you've landed a Lady Boss Princess, double huzzas for

you! Serve her well. Memorize the things you love her for and the ways in which she makes your life heavenly. And resolve that when you get to the big time you'll be the same sort of angel to the girls who work for you.

It's nice to talk about princesses but don't count on meeting one. Until more of the new-breed women get into the business world, there aren't enough to go around.

In ten years of hard labor I've met one Lady Boss Princess and about half a dozen super girl friends. So I can't be too encouraging. I can perhaps point out the problem ladies who still abound and tell you how I and others have coped. Let's start realistically with the more common varieties of Other Women.

The lady boss—witch version

If you've worked for one and come out unscarred, unscathed and still kicking, then she's probably one of those *rara aves* mentioned above. If you have yet to face a witch head on, be prepared for blood, sweat, toil and tears. The standard, straight-from-the-factory female executive without any of those fancy optional extras can take you for the most hair-raising ride on the track.

She may resent you if you're younger, prettier and more socially gregarious than she. She may mistreat you if you're quiet, yielding, placid and willing to take her guff. If she doesn't have a husband or lover or psychiatrist, she might try to take out her private frustrations on her obedient servant—you. She might be the perverse, sadistic sort who flaunts her status and her glamourous privileges, meanwhile reminding you that your lowly position is likely to last slightly short of forever.

The details of this grim character study haven't blossomed

full-blown from my imagination. They are distilled from the
sometimes painful, occasionally funny recollections of a few
women-run chain gangs on which I and others have done time.

The bitch-witch

Here's one Dora Dictator who would have driven Jung *and*
Adler to Freud's couch. She spent every waking moment on
guard against real or imagined slights. She was incredibly demanding of all around her. But to do her justice she was just
as demanding of herself—which is to say that she was a perfect
wizard at her job. A subordinate *could* learn the business from
her. But a five-day week tended to feel like thirty days on the
ocean floor without benefit of a decompression chamber. Everyone who went down into the deep with her contracted an
agonizing case of the bends. Many drowned.

Human qualities of forgiveness, understanding, kindness,
warmth or appreciation found no home in this woman. But she
was very definitely a woman—in fact, defensively, defiantly a
woman. Her eyes, her carriage and her voice were an open
dare to anyone who might question her femininity. The wild-
flower perfume, the clingy silk jersey dresses, the gracefully
crossed long legs, the flirty yet ladylike off-color stories, the
throaty laugh—all these could be turned on in a blinding flash
to mask the brutal, emasculating, power-mad Prussian under-
neath.

I have it on unimpeachable authority that in her more than
twenty years as a woman in charge of other women only two girls
worked for her for more than five months. I know one of the
two survivors, who clocked in at five months and two weeks. She
will never lose her battle scars. But she also will never equal the

education she received in professional expertise. On balance, she believes that the unspoken battle was worth the spoils.

Sometimes suffering pays off

In spite of everything, my reluctant, yet practical, advice is: don't throw down the gauntlet and don't throw in the sponge. Not if you basically enjoy the work you're doing. It's safe to say that a Lady Boss who makes the Wicked Witch of the West look like Mary Poppins must nevertheless have *something*. I mean, a lot of people had to tolerate her and value her all along the way or she wouldn't be in a position to make your life miserable. If she isn't the sister-in-law of the chairman of the board, she's most probably a dame with extraordinary talent, a razor-sharp business head (which went to her tongue) and a helluva lot to teach you despite herself.

Be charitable about her if humanly possible. She must have endured a lot of heat and flak to achieve her current status. Her hard shell may have been acquired to allow for her survival in a business jungle ruled by unsympathetic male predators.

Should this be your appraisal of your own situation, you might approach your witch this way: treat her as a woman and obey her as a man. You're clever enough to make the adjustment.

Rules of survival for the stalwart

Rule One: Praise her quietly and consistently but casually. Never act as though you are surprised by a bright idea of hers. Always act as though you expected brilliance from her and this latest campaign, sale, design, headline or whatever simply confirmed your expectations.

Rule Two: Maintain a stable mood. Never, never show that her criticism or current put-down has reached you. Do not cry in her presence no matter how anguished or humiliated you may be. Do not laugh too loudly. Pleasure makes this type of female break into hives.

Rule Three: Apologize profusely for even the tiniest of errors. *Never* make the same mistake (or even its distant relative) twice.

Rule Four: Do not dress too attractively. You might attract. She might get mad.

Rule Five: Ignore any signs or symptoms of her ups and downs. That includes hang-ups and letdowns. Let's say you noticed on her calendar that she had a personal date at 6:30 Tuesday night. Come Tuesday night you happen to be working late. You hear her in the next office pacing the floor, jumping to answer the phone when it rings—alas, it's for you, not her —and rushing to the entrance door of the office at the slightest sound—alas, it's the cleaning crew. By 7:30 it's obvious that she's been stood-up. Such a slight justifies capital punishment to this kind of woman. And if she can't get the man on the scaffold, her assistant will do just as well. Don't get sucked into the crisis. Oblivion is your keynote. Busyness is your cover. Make yourself scarce at all costs.

Rule Six: If you're younger than she is, cultivate a matronly appearance. I wore a schoolmarm bun low on the back of my head. And prayed that none of my own publishing friends would stray into the office unannounced. (In all honesty, as time wore on and my interesting lunch dates and cocktail meetings increased, I abandoned the bun. If she noticed, she didn't say anything.)

This may be too harsh, come to think of it. Especially so in today's youth-quake world. But if you're going the limit with a hard-core Lady Boss Witch you may have to make a stab at the bun bit or something comparable. Otherwise, if you find Rule Six *too much,* the hell with it.

The semiwitch

The Bitch Witch encompasses the worst of all possible evils. But take comfort. All my sources report that their experiences in bondage with Lady Bosses were nowhere near as grueling. Semiwitches run a broad spectrum and while life with them is no bed of bonus checks, it is considerably more tolerable. An "in-between" may have no more than one or two fatal flaws that will bug you every now and then. And though she's nothing compared to the package deal of misery that you get with the Bitch Witch, she can be plenty irritating if you've never known worse.

The witch in spite of herself

Take my first lady boss, for instance. She was the society-page editor on a small newspaper. My stint under her manicured thumb taught me a valuable lesson: you don't have to *get* personal with a lady boss to *have* personal problems. All I knew about this woman was that she was about fifty years old, had worked for the paper for twenty of those years, had children who were grown and married and a prosperous, respected husband. Her own family traced back to the Pilgrims and enjoyed a long history of friendship with the family that owned and published the newspaper.

You don't have to be a sociopsychological genius to recognize that this lady saw no threat in anyone who worked for her.

Younger women reminded her of her daughter. Newcomers to the city inspired her to act as any Mayflower American would to green immigrant stock—with benevolent maternalism. Her own solid security plus our lack of personal involvement with one another should have made this office an anteroom to heaven.

No such luck. From 8 A.M., when our day began, to 2:30 in the afternoon when the first edition of the day rolled off the presses, my boss was like a cook who fears the collapse of a soufflé before she has even whipped the egg whites. She checked and rechecked our stories the way compulsive housekeepers endlessly polish gleaming silverware. She was a tittering, flapping, entirely female nervous wreck. I could map her moods on graph paper to correspond with those maddening hot flashes which afflict many menopausal women.

During the summer that I worked for this newspaper editor, her menopause was *my* cross to bear.

I don't know how wildly imaginative *you* are. But I'm certain *I* would never have thought of middle-age menopause as a factor on my Lady Boss Warning Check List, if I hadn't lived through it firsthand. So take it for what it's worth. Even though I'll have to admit—and you'll be glad to hear it if you're reading this from a college dormitory—that the day of the twenty-six-year-old lady executive is right at hand. You may have to go some to become the chattel of a fiftyish Semi-witch whose hot flashes put you on the hot seat.

Midol can't cure everything

But there is a valid parallel to be made and emphasized. The twenty-six-year-old has something akin to hot flashes once every month. Depending on her biological legacy, it may mean anywhere from three to eight days of grumpsville for anyone who works for *her*.

A friend of mine has just such a monthly problem with her Lady Boss. My friend's solution is "If you can't beat it, chart it." She's probably the only executive assistant in town with her boss's menstrual cycle marked on her *own* calendar.

When your problem and hers is less clear-cut

So much for the physiological. Most of your hurdles are not going to be so easy to negotiate. When you work for a Lady Boss with a psychological or emotional hang-up, you can't solve it with a calendar or a biology textbook.

My friend Alice has weathered three women bosses in a field controlled by men at the very top but dominated by women on all the middle levels. Even in her responsible position, Alice herself still answers to a female superior. Alice considers her big Boss Lady to be basically tolerable—even a prize at times. But this boss can't qualify for princess status because of one major failing: she'll give Alice anything but money.

The root of all power

Alice has a secretary and two clerks. Alice gets introduced to all the right people. Alice gets full credit for everything she does. Alice travels for her company, goes to its most tony parties, attends the top-brass meetings. Alice looks for all the world like a $20,000-a-year success story, at the very least. But the ghastly truth is that, at age thirty-one, after three years as publicity director of a large swimwear firm, Alice earns $173.50

per week! Only her payroll clerk knows for sure—but Alice admitted it to me.

It seems that money is all the leverage this Boss Lady has with Alice. But it's enough. In an otherwise delightful working relationship, money keeps the tension high and the status line sharp and clear. And it's enough to make this lady executive a Semiwitch in Alice's eyes.

One of these weeks, Alice swears, she'll move on to more lucrative pastures. In the meantime, she's living rent free with a cousin, she's making valuable contacts on the job and she's learning like mad. Though underfed at the moment, Alice is nourished by a big, fat dream: she wants to work her way up to a job at a rival company. When she's earning double the salary that her boss is making she'll hire her ex-Boss Lady to work for her. Of such stuff are revenge fantasies made.

The green-eyed creature

Another friend has a Semiwitch Boss whose claws come out only when mutual men friends are involved. Ellen is an executive at a movie company. She's twenty-eight, she's lovely and she's not engaged—to be married, that is. Ellen *is* engaged in keeping half of the men in the industry in hot pursuit of her. But when she's not doing that and when she's not doing her job, Ellen is busy keeping her social life a deep dark secret from her green-eyed department head.

Ellen knows her boss's Achilles heel is spiked with jealousy. The boss, Angela, is ten years older than Ellen. Angela, an attractive divorcée with no children, is dedicated to her dating schedule. Her theory is that the bigger the pickings, the better the chance of a marriage proposal. She wants all the men to herself. Unfortunately, Angela fears that Ellen will find Mr.

Right first. Every one of Ellen's men friends is viewed as a potential husband snatched from Angela's grasp.

Ellen tells one anecdote to illustrate how her otherwise wonderful boss turns werewolf: "One day Angela brought up the subject of Marty, a motion-picture agent with whom both of us had had dealings. This man was just thirty. Too young for Angela I was sure. So when she asked if I had gone out with him I admitted that I had—a couple of times. I remained as noncommittal as possible, wondering all the time how she managed to discover that I had seen him socially. I was happy when the conversation turned to a script that Marty had submitted. Angela and I were on firm ground when talking business and I was relieved that we didn't sink into the quicksand of a let's-compare-men discussion.

"Several days later Angela called me into her office. She gave me a manuscript to read and then she said, 'By the way, I had a lovely evening with Marty last night. Dinner and the theatre and then drinks at my house until all hours.'

"What the hell do you say to a statement like that thrown at you clear out of the blue? I said: 'How nice,' and left it at that."

A glossary of lady bosses

We've covered only a smattering of tones in the Lady Boss spectrum from Princess through Semiwitch to Bitch-Witch and we still have barely scratched the surface.

Gird your loins and get out your geiger counter. Size up whether your Lady Boss is:

A "Can this Marriage Be Saved" reject who expects you to share her connubial woes.

A Jewish mother type who smothers you with protectiveness, reminds you to wear a muffler and checks up on your calorie count.

A displaced Dixiecrat whose slogan is "Me Master, You Slave," whether it's ten in the morning or eight at night.

A use-and-abuse type who thinks that your duties include mending her lace mantilla, picking up her prescription for birth-control pills or delivering a car muffler, by hand, to a recipient one hundred miles away.

A hard-up Hannah who expects you to fill her Saturday nights with whatever men you're not using at the moment.

A compulsive perfectionist who deals with her mistakes by blaming them on you.

An office politico who trusts you with secrets that you wish you never knew in the first place.

When you find yourself in a personal interview with a female executive, prepare to be at a disadvantage. She's got your resumé but you don't know where she's been and what she's done. She can check your references but you can rarely sound out other people's estimate of *her*. You may very well decide to give it a go—and the job offered to you may make it worth your while. But forewarned is forearmed.

Another "Other Woman" often found at the starting line-up of the offensive team is the Boss's Wife. Even if you take the preferred, safe route to the top, sticking steadfastly to male bosses, don't think you're going to escape the female touch. The Boss's Wife may live in Evanston but her poltergeist stalks the carpeted floor of your Chicago office.

Depending on the man you work for and the kind of marriage he and his wife maintain, the B.W. exerts anything from a constant influence to an occasional prod.

The wife is the last to know

As a secretary you may be placed in the role of official excuse maker-upper. Let's say the B.W. calls the office at ten to four and your boss still hasn't come back from lunch. You know that he went to the Oak Room with that gorgeous sales representative from Revlon. You also know that he left the office at 12:30. And it occurs to you that the Oak Room is a restaurant in the Plaza Hotel and that hotels are well known for having bedrooms on their upper floors and that your boss is well known for his extracurricular activities.

So you're on the telephone with the wife and she's saying something like, "My heavens, it's nearly four and he's not back yet?"

If you've got smarts, you *won't* tell it like it is. You'll think fast, sound sincere and in your most casual, secretarial voice you'll say something like, "Well, he had a lunch date with someone from Revlon and I know that after that he wanted to stop in at the Cosmetics Trade Exhibit."

The B.W. will swallow it whole. You'll have spared her from being hurt (he's doing a good-enough job of it without *your* help). And your boss will adore you not only for the fib but for furnishing him with a sensible, credible excuse.

This is a tough game to play but in my opinion it's bigger than both of you. I've heard two main bodies of opinion on the secretary's role as lead liar. One says that the boss has no right to make you run interference for his philandering and you shouldn't compound his mendacity with your own. The other opinion holds that you have no right to be the bearer of painful truths. Your cover-ups are white lies, which in a sense are more protective of the B.W. than they are of the blackguard you call boss. I stand with the latter.

Guard duty

Still, if this peculiar service is expected of you, your boss owes it to you to feed you the stories he wants the wife to hear. He doesn't have to get you in a huddle and detail a game plan of his indiscretions in order to prepare you for guard duty. He can put up his own front to save both of you embarrassment. Let him lie to you—even though it's as obvious as the Scotch on his breath—so that you can carry his fib directly to the wife. Asking you to manufacture a Cosmetics Trade Exhibit on the spot twice a week is demanding ingenuity beyond the call of duty.

If you're at all like me, i.e., a hopeless square about the sanctity of marriage—you may resent being raked into these shenanigans in the first place. Then, you have to decide whether a long talk with your boss—but only about your role in the deceit, not a lecture on morals—would do any good. If not, your next step would have to be out the door. Your voluntary exit is the most likely resolution of this problem, if it is a problem for you.

Scarsdale research

Some men don't talk very much to their wives, especially about their business. Some wives aren't interested in the grisly details of buy and sell orders, the Standard Rate and Data report on WBGA radio or rising trucking rates on the Baltimore-to-Miami run. Some businesses are just not cut out for dinner-table discussion. Nuclear physics, actuarial tables and plumbing come immediately to mind.

But in many families, the husband's working experiences are carried home to the wife faster than any interoffice memo can circulate. If the wife has no job of her own, no kids at home and has help with the household chores, then you have the most fertile possible ground for what has become known as Scarsdale Research.

Here's the way it works: the boss has a problem. In my boss's case, it's often a book in search of a title. Once it was the autobiography of King Hussein of Jordan. We had editorial meetings galore. The author-collaborator was bereft of inspiration. We went through all of King Hussein's correspondence but no phrases popped out and cried, "Title!" Someone checked Bartlett's *Familiar Quotations*. Finally our boss, Bernard Geis, came in one morning with what was clearly THE ideal title for a book about the plucky and beleaguered young monarch in the Middle East. The Hussein book was now *Uneasy Lies the Head*. The primary source, of course, was Shakespeare's "Uneasy lies the head that wears a crown." But someone had to be smart enough to borrow the quote and turn it into a title, and that someone didn't work in our office.

Cries of "brilliant" and "How did you ever think of it!" echoed around the office.

Because Bernard Geis is a hopelessly honest man, he came right out with it. "It came to me in a flash," he said. "I knew it was the perfect title the minute Darlene told it to me."

Mrs. Geis happened to contribute something that we all thought valid and usable. Which she often does. You may not be as blessed. The Little Lady who stands behind your Big Boss is probably the last person you'd call upon for an opinion. But your boss goes home to Scarsdale every night bursting with the day's doings and she is full of pat solutions to every problem from personnel to how to market Man Tan in equatorial Africa. Whether she is an advertising genius hiding under an apron or whether she's a dumb-dumb who has your boss by the nose, you're likely to get the B.W.'s point of view along about coffee-break time in the morning. You won't need a scorecard to see where his opinions end and hers begin. But if he's not Bernard Geis he's most likely going to pass it all off as original thinking.

You have two options as I see it: you can play it his way and agree or disagree with him as you normally would, regardless of whose stamp is on each idea; or you can blast away at the portions of his spiel that you have a hunch came from Scarsdale the night before. If they're bad enough you'll have an easy job isolating *her* contributions. Then he may have to own up under the onslaught and blame the faulty thinking on his wife (with an embarrassed chuckle and a "you know how it is") and that may be the last you see of her absentee landlord participation in your professional bailiwick.

The loneliness of the long-distance wife

Wives who are not on the scene can play other roles besides the Scarsdale Research walk-on parts. Hiring, admiring, retiring and firing are often the specialties of the Boss's Wife.

Enough jokes have been made about wives' objections to good-looking office girls that beating this particular triangle has become a monotone. But as with most durable forms of humor, such as mother-in-law jokes and traveling salesman stories, these are funny and evocative precisely because of their foundation in truth.

One *can* empathize with the Boss's Wife. She's helpless, she's frustrated and she's far away. But the situation can be equally trying for an ambitious girl in business who can't help it if she happens to look like a Penn State Homecoming Queen.

The boss is impaled on the horns of a sticky dilemma: should he defer to his wife's jealous demands or should he succumb to his natural desire for a qualified and also diverting female subordinate, whether she be a secretary or underling executive? However faithful and devoted a husband he may be, the notion of a pretty young thing decorating his outer office is undeniably appealing. A bright and beautiful Parisienne research assistant can be just as much a business asset as a French Provincial office décor.

The CIA wife

At one large publishing house the very top man—publisher and founder of the empire—did not allow his wife's influence to pervade the editorial or business side of the operation. But her vigilant scrutiny of company women was the talk of the trade. This B.W. provided Mr. Publisher with a long line of male secretaries. She laid down strict ground rules for the advancement of female editors, department heads and executives. It was really as simple as it was inflexible: any executive position that placed a woman in direct contact with Mr. Publisher must be filled by the old, the infirm, the unattractive, the neuter or the confirmed and condemned spinster.

Otherwise, his spouse, who operated as a long-distance Boss's Wife *par excellence,* would have had to worry about sales conferences, editorial meetings, promotion and advertising confabs and company picnics. By eliminating the possibility of diverting ladies she eliminated the need for everyday spy work.

Further refinements of her theories about personnel went something like this: other men's secretaries within the firm were the worry of the other men's wives. Since Mr. Publisher rarely went for a dip in the typing pool, his only dealings were with the various male bosses and vice presidents and the few carefully screened lady executives who had already passed the B.W.'s own security clearance.

One notable exception slipped through the screening process in the late 1950s. Her story is legendary. Marsha was a sophisticated, statuesque Vassar graduate who started in the company as secretary to the executive editor. Hired the same day was Jim, a bright witty young man who was to serve as the editor's assistant.

After two years of departmental bliss this *bureau à trois* was torn asunder by the death of the executive editor. In due course the other two moved up a notch—Jim became a full-fledged editor and Marsha his editorial assistant.

Even if Mrs. Publisher had noticed Marsha's promotion it wouldn't yet have qualified her for expulsion. Marsha wasn't upper level enough. And far from the maddening crowd of authors, agents and *literati,* Mrs. Publisher did not notice that Marsha was making herself marvelously indispensable. Jim gave Marsha editorial assignments, took her on lunch dates, and turned over some prestigious authors to her care. She became the editor and confidante of a famous philosopher. She signed up a British essayist. She brought into the house two first novelists, one of whom produced the fiction best seller of the year. The other fell madly and openly in love with her.

Cold swan, warm heart

On the publication date of his book, the novelist sent up to the office a five-foot-tall sculpture of a swan, carved entirely of ice and wheeled in on a brass wagon. Frozen into the center of the sculpture was a love letter for Marsha.

We all knew that Marsha's star was on the rise. But it never glittered so brightly or shone so proudly as on the day that *Newsweek* magazine ran her picture, along with the novelist's, as part of a feature story on his book. That was the day before the day that Marsha was fired.

Her title hadn't changed. Her salary was still the same modest assistant's salary it had been the day before. But Marsha had broken Mrs. Publisher's cardinal rule: No woman was to be *publicly* associated with the firm unless that woman was Mrs. Publisher. Period. No "buts" about it except for the butts that got the heave ho for doing otherwise. How could Mr. Publisher be so weak and pusillanimous as to let this happen to a perfectly innocent, talented and valuable executive? I can only answer by saying you'd have to meet Mrs. Publisher to understand.

Marsha's abrupt dismissal left rumor and truth to fend for themselves. I can't swear that Marsha's dismissal went like this but the following account has survived a decade intact. It seems that Mrs. Publisher told Mr. Publisher that Marsha had been "sleeping around" with authors of the firm and "using her sex" to get favorable contracts from agents and generally reflecting disgrace upon the company name. And on top of everything, Marsha wore couturier clothes! Mr. Publisher didn't quite understand the final charge in the indictment, but less unworldly executives in his organization understood it only too well. Mrs. Publisher prided herself on her expensive designer wardrobe. How dare a mere slip of an employee compete with her! Marsha, in her black Balenciaga, was given a pink slip for her sins, which existed nowhere but in the B.W.'s malicious mind.

Book publishing's loss was magazine publishing's gain. Marsha is now a top editor on a major women's monthly. At last report she was "using her sex" for nothing more salacious than editing spicy recipes.

Possessive, peculiar and persnickety Bosses' Wives can be a nasty irritant. Something like a blister on the foot: hard to ignore, miserable to live with, but easy to treat. Put on a pair of comfortable shoes, loosen the laces and start walking.

Secretaries make the best "other" women—or the worst

How you feel about secretaries depends upon which side of the fence you're on at any given moment. And with this particular sticky picket fence, there are not two sides, there are three.

Either you *are* a secretary. Or you *have* a secretary. Or someone else's secretary has *you*—in a spot. Your experiences as a secretary on the winding road to fame and fortune in a man's world are not the valid concern of this chapter on Other Women in your life.

The care and feeding of your own secretary is a big and crucial subject which I have discussed earlier and will discuss again. And I still shall not have exhausted its possibilities or its ramifications.

But other people's secretaries! There's a subject guaranteed to arouse extremes of bile or bliss in everyone I've questioned. And for many a good reason.

The interventionist

Other people's secretaries can be invaluable gems to the people they work for, but to you they are often Scylla and

Charybdis combined. Most anyone of rank that you deal with in business has a secretary who clears his telephone calls and checks out his visitors. If your name is unknown to the secretary she'll screen you, quiz you, beleaguer you with "I'm sure *I* can be helpful" until you feel like resorting to Western Union to reach her boss. There are variations, but the basic Interventionist Tactic is fairly common.

Recently, I tried to call a prominent author-critic who also teaches at a New York university. I was connected to his office on campus where his phone was "manned" by a stalwart secretary with an Irish accent. (British-accented secretaries are even more unnerving, persevering *and* prevalent.) Here's a more or less literal reconstruction of the whole bloody conversation:

Me: Hello. This is Letty Cottin Pogrebin at Bernard Geis Associates. May I speak with the professor?

She: He's busy preparing for his next class. May *I* help you?

Me: Well, it's rather complicated. If you don't mind I would prefer not to go over it twice. Would it be all right if I called back after his class, at say, ten past one?

She: I'm so sorry but his afternoon schedule is quite tight with appointments. Why don't you give me an idea of your business and I'll pass it along to him.

Me: That's kind of you. But it's something I will have to discuss with the professor. When do you think would be a convenient time to call?

She: I'll just have to know what you're calling about.

Me: Yes, I know that you can't relay every call to the professor. However, this is in regard to a review which I understand he has prepared for publication in *The New York Review of Books.*

She: Oh? On what book?

Me: Must I really go into the whole matter with you now?

She: You can be sure I'll furnish the professor with the information.

Me: (*In partial defeat*) The book is *Six Seconds in Dallas.* The author is Professor Josiah Thompson. The subject is the assassination of President Kennedy.

She: *Six Seconds in Dallas?* Oh, yes. He's read it.

Me: I *know* he's read it! I sent him the complimentary advance copy of the book. And I know he's done this review. And there are some peripheral matters, some recent legal developments connected to the book's publication of which I am sure he will want to be made aware. Now *would* you let me know a good time to call the professor back? Perhaps between appointments? Or after his last class? Or sometime tomorrow?

She: Oh, the professor *never* discusses his reviews with anyone until they have been published.

Me: Click.

If you can't beat 'em, hang up on 'em. This woman was utterly invincible. With all due respect to this author-critic-professor and with full appreciation of the number of unimportant, irrelevant, if not crank, phone calls he receives, I am convinced that he is *not* being properly served by this stubborn guardian. I know that my call would have been of considerable interest to him. I know this because with the aid of five or six friends of friends I did get the information to him eventually and he used it in his review. But his secretary's overzealous protectiveness almost killed all chance of communication.

Secretaries have little opportunity to feel important. Naturally they hunger for some small sense of power. I think it's healthy to participate in one's boss's affairs to some extent. But operating as a one-woman Legion of Decency is indecent.

Often it's the unexpected phone call or the out-of-the-blue caller who bears the best tidings. If the boss gets neither the call itself nor the message about the call, a secretary can be unwittingly responsible for the loss of untold friends or opportunities.

A secretary with a secret

On the more frivolous side of the coin, we have to cope with secretaries whose romantic interest in their bosses creates an even more complex clearance procedure. When a secretary calls her boss *Mister* Harris and everyone knows they've been sleeping together for two years—and everyone else calls him Willie—you can be sure that's a secretary who will stand between her boss and the world to her dying breath.

The best way to get past this shield and sword protectress is to establish early in the game that you are (a) happily married or (b) deeply involved with some man somewhere or (c) *very, very* businesslike or (d) too important to play games with.

My friend Liz has been trying since September to make a business lunch appointment with a certain television producer. It's now December. His secretary reports very coolly and formally that his lunch times are booked up through March. She suggests that Liz make a note on her calendar to check back around Easter. I have serious doubts that even Richard Nixon is busy every noontime between now and next Easter. Liz has even more serious doubts that this producer knows she has ever called at all.

Because I've become such a nut on the subject of secretarial interference I stopped having my own secretary clear my calls. It used to be that the receptionist answered, "Bernard Geis Associates" and then if the call was for me it was relayed to my secretary, who answered, "Mrs. Pogrebin's office," and then, if I felt like it, I took the call.

This was a pure pain and a waste of time for anyone on the other end of the telephone. It also finally struck me as a pretentious formality. A caller would have every right to suspect that when my secretary claimed I was not in, I was really using her as a dodge. After all, my girl would say, "Who's calling please?" and *after* receiving the person's name, she would either report that I would speak to the caller or that I was not in.

Since I started taking all my calls direct from the switchboard I may have lost an hour a month in aimless and irrelevant conversation I would formerly have avoided. But I haven't lost any friends or insulted any incipient acquaintances. And my secretary isn't bugging anyone the way some other people's secretaries bug me.

Two immovable objects

A variation of this Interventionst Secretary is the girl who will not allow her boss to suffer the indignity of getting on the phone with another secretary. My idea of telephone etiquette is that having my secretary make calls for me is proper so long as I promptly respond when my party is on the phone. Yet many times my enthusiastic "Hello, Hymie!" is chilled by an icy "One moment please, I'll connect you."

The ultimate breakdown in communication is achieved when an Interventionist Secretary makes a call for her boss to someone equally blessed with an Interventionist Secretary. The resultant clash has come to be known as "Whose boss gets on first." And if the secretaries are similarly determined, the call may never be completed.

As with Lady Bosses and Bosses' Wives, there are some

priceless secretaries deserving of loud kudos. I have found several who are more sensible, responsible and knowledgeable than their bosses. Two New York radio shows are put together by very harried, curt, nervous producers. I've learned over the years not to even bother asking for them. I book the author via the secretaries who are superefficient dolls. Both of these girls should, by rights, have their bosses' jobs. Let's hope that they read this book and become inspired to leave their voluntary servitude behind them.

The even-more-aggressive-than-you girl

She's the crew member who's dying to turn in her oars for a captain's cap. She comes on like a workhorse but every moment that she's pulling the plow, she's plotting how to make it to the Preakness, the Belmont and the Kentucky Derby all within the next six months. If you're even mildly perceptive, it won't take you long to learn what makes this Sally run.

If you haven't the stomach or the spirit to play it her way, sit tight and let her pass you on this move. Or shove off to greener pastures and less omnivorous fillies. A prudent dose of aggressiveness is a healthy accompaniment to ambition. But it shouldn't provide immunity to other people's feelings. It shouldn't inure you to the wounds a claw-baring woman can inflict while scratching her way to the same goal you have in mind.

The even-more-agressive-than-you-girl is most useful to you as a negative example. *You* needn't sink so low. Women's office politics are messy, irrational hornet's nests. Often the goal of all that fussing and buzzing is not a promotion or a raise but just a sting for sting's sake.

A friend who is an assistant buyer in a large department store puts it this way:

"Most of our crawling and clawing is motivated by petty status worries. Will she get a secretary before I do? Or why should she have a window in her office when mine is just an airless crypt? Or how come Mary can take the Directional salesman to lunch and I haven't a lousy penny for an expense account?

"It's tiresome and sickening to keep looking over your shoulder to make sure none of the other girls is overtaking you. It reminds me of being a kid playing musical chairs. I always ended up with a knot in my stomach whether or not I got to sit in a chair when the music stopped."

Another girl who works for a women's magazine says her office musical chairs is more like a childhood game called King of the Mountain. There's the editor in chief securely sitting on top of the mountain and all his girl assistants and lady editors scrambling up the hillside trying to get close to him. Women sell their souls and their pride for a pat on the head from the king figure. At this magazine, job titles are jealously guarded. Women make more a fuss about titles than about a $5-a-week raise. When the secretary becomes an editorial assistant and her name goes on the magazine's masthead, her colleague secretaries nurse their wounds for weeks.

When my friend received a dispensation from the editor in chief to have her office painted, one of her colleagues, another senior editor, couldn't face the staff because *her* office wasn't approved for a paint job. She came in one weekend and with her brother's help she painted the place herself. Now she swears up and down that the authorization *did* come through—only a bit late.

The aggressive coworker can occasionally rile even the most benign of us into retaliatory thrusts. But no matter how aroused your jousting spirit may get, bear in mind that those who consort with thieves usually end up with a criminal record. If you once saved the life of the police commissioner's son, then maybe you can consort. Otherwise, you would be better advised to protect your reputation and shun the poisonous tactics of the more carnivorous career girls in your midst.

The nice nellie

Here's a breed of Other Woman who is sometimes tough to spot. She may not be carnivorous but she's a wolf in sheep's clothing nonetheless. Overtly pleasant, inside she's really a teeming mass of frustration, inadequacies and self-hatred. She's the nonaspiring coworker who has appointed herself judge and jury of your motives and behavior. By taking herself out of the running she feels justified in providing an "impartial" sideline commentary on your progress.

She started right beside you and is going no further. She's decided to remain a big fish in the little typing pool and she damns you for daring to be a little fish in the big pond. She's first to remind you that you're still a tadpole or to point out that barracudas eat their young.

She sounds helpful, she looks helpful, she acts helpful—but it's a studied and devious camouflage. Her soft-gloved hand encloses a stiletto.

Beware of her advice. Shun her "helpful" criticism. Otherwise you'll start believing that your perfectly normal, all-American ambition is rank Machiavellian cunning.

Since this type fools the eye, you'll have to develop a supersensitive ear. To launch your audio perceptiveness, here are some classic lines that identify a Nice Nellie as a Vera Viper:

What She Says	*What She Means*
"Are you really going to wear that knit dress to the annual meeting? Don't you think it's too revealing?"	That dress is sensational! You'll steal the spotlight from all of us.
"You'd better think twice about going to Cleveland with the boss. He may behave himself around the office but you never know. Five hundred miles can bring out the beast in him."	Why didn't he ask me to go?
"That picture of you in the company magazine was lovely. It's too bad your roots were showing that day."	How come you get all the attention? I've never had my picture in *anything*.
"Congratulations on your promotion. Of course, if you want to be one of those career girls you're really on your way. Personally, I'm more interested in men and marriage."	You really have it made. I didn't get the promotion and I don't even have a date for Saturday night.
"I just hope those lawyers don't want an affidavit from me. They've gotten you terribly involved in the case."	You're so lucky to be a part of the most fascinating copyright case on record. Why don't they want my testimony? I work here too.

The botchers or don't-give-a-damns

These ladies with forked tongues are commonplace hurdles in the unobtrusive obstacle course of Other Women. But you may sufficiently control your own fate to sidestep them once you've seen their true colors. A word should be said about the ones you can't do anything about such as lady personnel managers (who see on your resumé that you majored in comparative literature and promptly send you to be interviewed for a bookkeeper job); or lady employment agents (invariably polished, marbles-in-the-mouth snits who dispatch you in senseless rounds of interviews with half an eye on your job interests and six eyes on the agency fee); or indifferent office clerks (who always mange to file your most important contract in some folder marked for oblivion).

These women can't be helped . . . and probably they can't help themselves. Their inefficiency or ineptitude can make your work look lousy or your life seem needlessly complicated. Recommended antidote: Don't delegate jobs, do it yourself. Don't depend on those with unproven ability, do it yourself. Don't count on other people being as interested in a job well done, do it yourself.

Lesbian ladies

Girls who like girls—too much—are a sad, often desperate lot. The vernacular has dubbed them butches (the tough, male-emulating kind) and femmes (they play the standard girl's role). I've only known two in the publishing business and both are fairly well acknowledged because they are the butch type. Short, boyish (not Sassoon-y) hairdos, a clodding walk, deep voice, blunt nails and excessively tailored clothes are their trademarks. But these two dames don't practice any trade, except the business of publishing. They are not predatory beasts lurking near the water cooler, waiting for the first freckle-faced Rebecca of Sunnybrook Farm that they can lure into a life of single-sexed sin.

You may be ten feet from an honest-to-goodness lesbian every business day and never know it. As a general rule, they are the closet variety. They live by night. And it seems only fair that they should be able to "pass" during the day. Everyone has to make a living.

The casting couch sexpert

I've saved her for last because I'm almost sure that she is a dying species. And it's kind of silly to make a ruckus about a threat who is on the brink of extinction.

But there are some holdouts, I'm told. The Casting Couch Sexpert is not just indigenous to Hollywood. She has a counterpart on Madison Avenue and Wall Street and from Boston to Big Sur.

It's easy to say, "If you can't beat her join her in the game." But the stakes are too high. Sex is too available nowadays to be used as dependable barter, no matter how expendable you consider your virtue. The sexpert status seeker may triumphantly zoom past you up the executive ladder—but you'll live to trip over her on *her* way down.

A case history worth pondering came to me via Connie, the beneficiary of the happy ending. Connie and Helene were both media research assistants at a major Four-A advertising agency. They worked under a lady media director who was pregnant and had recently given two months' notice that she was leaving to be a full-time mother. The vice president in charge of media had not begun to interview for a replacement. Both Connie and Helene had hopes that the v.p. might give one of them a crack at the director's job.

Connie felt that she should have had the edge over Helene because of an extra year's experience in both media and traffic. But Connie was not oblivious to Helene's advantage. Helene had woven an obvious spell over the vice president. He was virtually gaga over her. Even before the media director had turned up reading Dr. Spock, Helene was clearly the vice president's fair-haired lass. He was always perched on the edge of her desk, peeking into her ever-present décolletage neckline, finding excuses for after-hour assignments for her and generally making a spectacle of himself.

Connie felt powerless in the face of this libidinal chemistry. She couldn't fight fire with fire because she had neither the disposition nor the cleavage to do the trick.

As the media director's two months' notice went into its final week, Connie started looking for another job. To confirm her feeling that Helene was going to get the promotion, Connie witnessed a lovey-dovey lunch scene between Helene and the vice president in a dark corner of a restaurant. The cooing and kissing was an unmistakable signal that sex was going to decide the issue.

Four days later, as Connie was leaving the building at the end of the day, Helene rushed up to her in a state of tearful hysteria. The vice president had given her her walking papers. Helene just *had* to talk it off her chest. The two girls repaired to a nearby pub and over double martinis Helene bitched about her double cross. She had done everything—"and I do mean *everything*"—for that man and he pays her off with a lousy check for three weeks' severance.

As Helene saw it, the vice president couldn't resist her charms but once he possessed them in the flesh, he couldn't ignore the belated clarion call of conscience. "A guilt-stricken married man is like a wounded bull," Helene announced. "The bastard just couldn't face me. He said I reminded him of his moral weakness. As long as I worked at the agency he would never be able to forget!"

Connie was properly sympathetic. She sat with Helene until the martinis dulled her rival's outrage and then she left the bar. The very next day, hard-working, nose-to-the-grindstone Connie, whose most décolletage blouse was a cowl-neck jersey, was offered a six-month trial period as media director. That was four years ago. Today, Connie's business card reads "media director" and her higher status has not lowered her neckline.

Well, our tour of the office powder room is complete. Despite the warnings and despite the gory details of our ladies' day in a man's world, don't be dismayed. While you're down there looking up, other women in business are naturally going to seem outsized and formidable. The successful executive you admire and envy will seem to be Wonder Woman in a Chanel suit. It's all in your perspective.

Once on your way, with a challenging, diverting job to occupy your every working moment, you won't have the time, interest or patience for Other Woman Watching. You'll be amazed at how convivial relationships become when the big job replaces the petty rivalries. That's when lower level all-girl machinations and miseries fade into memory. That's when women you meet are just like you—bright, dedicated, enthusiastic, and fun to have around.

5.

The men in your life

*T*he great thing about getting along with men is that it requires so little work. Compared to the adjustments you must make and the careful psychology you must use to cope with females, manhandling is a piece of cake. As an unabashed man fan, I feel qualified to make some broad-based generalizations at the outset: most men are emotionally honest and uncomplicated; they are professionally realistic and straightforward; they are not devious or malicious in their personal relations no matter how practiced they may be at sharp business tactics; men are usually dependable confidants, lavish with praise, fair-minded and seven and a half times out of ten they have fascinating intellects, interests or opinions.

If you disagree with this sweeping profile then you haven't met enough men. All the more reason for you to worm your way into a man's world with zest and high anticipation.

If you're single you can't be blamed for viewing every human being who shaves and wears long pants as a possible husband. But try for a moment to suppress this natural instinct. I can't offer a Baedecker for the predatory female. I never perfected a flip, index-card system for the classification of the male of the species according to his habits and markings. Even before I was married I don't recall that I ever checked off male acquaintances into two categories: groom or gloom. I probably made this determination unconsciously. But the main point is that I never discriminated against a man because he was *not* eligible marriage material. And I can't disagree loudly enough with the breezy magazine articles that counsel you to join the working class just to find a mate.

The incorrigible husband hunter

A friend of mine is on this husband-hunting treadmill and can't get off. Instead of meeting her boss's clients in a relaxed, friendly manner she carries on as if each one were a blind date for *her*. Her boss is a big theatrical lawyer whose friends and clients run the gamut from millionaire producers to struggling actors, from angels who back Broadway shows to borsht-belt comedians. A fascinating admixture of humanity passes my friend's desk and she, as a very capable personal secretary and administrative assistant to the lawyer, has ample opportunity to meet and get to know all of them—mostly men. She could collect these unusual people as friends the way some people collect foreign postage stamps that come their way. She could establish relationships which would yield her infinite rewards: intangible ones like a real inside view of the workings of show business and tangible ones like free tickets to an opening night.

Is she the toast of Shubert Alley? Is she the livest wire on the cocktail-party circuits? Nope. She's just an uptight husband-hungry gal whose eyes light up every time a new client comes in the door. But when the client turns out to be seventy-two years old and paunchy or when he flashes pictures of his kids those same eyes film over and nearly clamp shut. To my friend, a man who is not eligible to become lover or husband is an invisible man.

The men she considers "possibles" set all her predatory machinery in motion. She flirts, she teases, she practically advertises her availability in neon lights. She fantasizes that married men will eventually leave their wives for her. She imagines that homosexual actors will revise their sexual proclivities for her. She convinces herself that her Prince Charming is going to come to the office in search of a lawyer and that he will find his Cinderella instead.

She's been at it for four years now—though how her boss has put up with her antics is beyond me—and it hasn't netted her much more than a half-dozen dates for all her efforts. Who can count the interesting friendships she has missed by turning to ice whenever a client's intentions are not romantic? Worst of all, she isn't even enjoying her job. The tensions produced by constantly pressing the *femme fatale* button have sapped this girl's energies. She may be on the make. But she sure isn't making it. And she isn't making men like being around her when the deep freeze sets in.

Ergo, the ego

Men do sometimes have to get special treatment that requires extra effort and feminine sensitivity. This has nothing to do with hunting them down, trapping them, capturing them or putting one over on them. As I see it, some men have to be "handled" sometimes because beneath the thick skin of the stronger sex lies an open wound called the Male Ego.

Don't get me wrong. I mean this as a statement of truth, not as a putdown. Matter of fact, I love the Male Ego. It's what makes a guy confident, proud, charming, funny and clever. A man who likes himself makes it easy for others to like him. A healthy ego puts others at ease. It allows a man to make a speech before three hundred buyers at a convention when he has never before spoken to an audience greater than two: his mother and his dog. It's what inspires a man to dress smartly, to walk tall or to ask you out to dinner even though you may be the most beautiful girl he's ever seen.

Needless to say, too much ego makes Jack a swaggering fool and too little makes him pitiable. But Mr. Average with an everyday Male Ego is still occasionally very vulnerable. Think of the Male Ego as a helium balloon which keeps a man buoyant, bouncy and jaunty-jolly. The balloon is just fine if it is given an occasional pumping up with words of praise or a bonus or a killing on the stock market. However, it collapses sadly at the slightest pinprick. Here are some classic ego deflators:

> His girl friend gets drunk at a party and announces that he's lousy in bed.

> His wife gets talky at a dinner party at the boss's house and she brags that her husband helps her with the ironing.

> His secretary lets loose with the news that he always takes tranquilizers before board meetings.

> His boyhood friend, newly hired by the firm, delights in telling colleagues how his old pal was the neighborhood weakling who sent away for the Charles Atlas course.

> His wife brags at the office picnic that his latest merchandising brainstorm was really *her* idea.

When dealing with a man in the business world it's wise to bear in mind that he may have recently suffered such assault on his ego. If so, he was very possibly scratched by female claws. He may be having a tough time reinflating. He's not going to appreciate any big-shot tactics from the soft little you sitting across the conference table. As a girl—and particularly if you're youngish—you may have to prove to a man that you're knowledgeable, well informed in your field and experienced at the job in question. But you don't have to outsmart him. Handling a man is nothing more than protecting his ego. And if you're an intuitive female with reasonable sensitivity, then protecting his ego is nothing more than appreciating him *overtly* as a man— for what he says, for what he does, for how he does it and for the way that he makes you feel.

I once had dealings with an advertising executive who was very short. In fact, he was wee. No more than five foot one with shoes on. The mind boggles when imagining the ego indignities this fellow must have suffered throughout his life. During our many conversations I learned that he was married to a woman who, he proclaimed, was half a foot taller than he; that he had two children who, the pediatrician had announced, were "very tall for their ages"; that he played a neat game of basketball despite his "height disadvantage." You couldn't miss his hang-up if you tried.

I liked the man. I found it effortless to please him and to dissipate his defensiveness. All I did was focus on his work. He'd done some brilliant ads for other publishers. I remembered them vividly and told him so. He turned out a superlative campaign for us. I raved over it. He was a big man in my eyes because he had a big talent. I didn't have to mention that my husband was six feet tall. I didn't have to stand up when we worked on layouts because then he would have had to look *up* at me. A little bit of handling went a long way. We had a pleasant working friendship—two people with a common interest, not a five-foot-one man versus a five-foot-four woman.

All egos are not alike, obviously. And handling a man is not something that can be put in recipe form. Most of your energies should be focused on being your best self, with just a passing awareness of the Male Ego whenever you feel it necessary to step lightly in the presence of that fragile balloon we visualized at the beginning of this discussion.

Come to think of it, being your *best self* is really the key to success with men as much as it is the key to your personal and professional success.

Equal treatment for all

A consistent outflow of the best that's in you is not as depleting or as enervating as it may sound. Who knows? Top form may become standard operating procedure if you practice it on everybody. When you're coruscating and charming to the top brass and you're a cold bitch to the mailboy, someone is bound to trap you in your duplicity. And besides, it's a strain to put people through a sort of Checkpoint Charlie for Status before you decide which personality to turn on. If snobbery is okay in its place, and I doubt it, that place is certainly not in an office. The *fact* of your position is enough to differentiate you from the rank and file. There's absolutely no need to compound the injury with aloofness to your lessers or by bootlicking your betters.

Just as that kingdom in antiquity was lost for want of a nail to shoe a horse to carry a rider to wage a battle to win a war—so your biggest, hottest deal can be lost for want of a friendly mailboy. It would be foolish to cultivate every cog in the wheel of business just in case you need a future favor. Nevertheless, a warm sensitivity to all the people you deal with is sure to repay you some day in time of need.

A girl I know was a prime apple polisher toward superiors and an incorrigible phony big shot to all the little guys around the office. She didn't realize the truth in our motto: never

underestimate the power of the Xerox machine operator. Until
the day that she needed a copy made of a reader's report
stolen from a motion-picture company's inner-sanctum files. A
boy friend had slipped the report to her with the proviso that
she have it back in his hands within fifteen minutes. It was
two pages long. Her secretary was out to lunch, and in any case
it would have been difficult to type a copy and still return
the document to meet the imposed deadline. My friend rushed
to the Xerox room. She was savoring the glory that would be hers
by presenting the pilfered secret report at the next executive
meeting. The report gave a clear indication of the movie
company's high expectations for the book that was under consideration. In fact, there was even a paragraph recommending
that the producer buy the property "at almost any price."
Needless to say, this was a coup and a half for my friend.
Armed with this inside information, our publisher could hold
out for a high six-figure price for a novel that he originally
had no intention of selling to Hollywood for more than fifty
thousand dollars—if he was lucky.

So my friend dashed up to the Xerox machine, shoved the
report under the machine operator's nose and ordered, "Three
copies right away, please."

But her chickens had come home to roost. The young man
had worked up such a resentment to this posturing, self-inflated
girl that he had decided to call a private sit-down strike.
"Sorry, the machine's on the blink," he answered.

"Oh, but you *must* get it going immediately. I've got to have
a copy of this right away."

"It don't budge," the boy said impassively. "Have to call
Xerox and get a serviceman over here, I guess."

"Young man, I haven't got time for a serviceman. One copy
will do. Surely you can squeeze even one lousy, blurred copy
out of this goddam monster." She was betraying her desperation.

He whistled, fiddled with a few dials, pressed a button or two and simply shrugged his shoulders.

She pleaded, whined, implored and begged him to try to fix the duplicator. The more frantic she became, the more resolute and self-satisfied was the boy. His turn had come. Salary, status and pride melted away in this confrontation. They were in the Xerox room, on his home court and the game was his.

The girl consulted her watch nervously. She saw her opportunity eke away with the minutes. She barely had time to return to her desk to scribble a few of the key phrases from the report so that she could at least capture the essence of it for her bosses. But the big chance was lost. Nothing would carry the weight that the lifted document itself would have.

As she left the Xerox room and ran down the hall she heard, in utter disbelief, the loud even hum of the Xerox motor and the healthy click-click as it fed out copies of somebody's papers. The boy was whistling an unrecognizable triumphant tune.

A Xerox operator may be just one fellow in the magnificent galaxy of mankind in a girl's professional universe. But be he the sun about which her life and livelihood revolve or a small passing comet, she can and should shine as brightly for both.

The boss

I have had, by rapid count, nine male bosses—some direct supervisors and some top-echelon head men who were president, director, owner of the company or otherwise in charge of the action. Each of them was as different from the other as nine random people might be expected to be. Those character and personality differences did determine my relationship with each man. So too did my various responsibilities dictate my behavior and the boss's reactions to me. But beneath it all certain consistencies are worth noting—if only because I was never fired and because I count almost all of the men as good friends or friendly acquaintances to this day. There was one early boss who *didn't* feel that I hung out the moon. He never forgave me for not being a Republican. And I wasn't too respectful of his conservative views. But the other eight men and I got along famously. So I must have been doing *something* right.

Some of my best friends are bosses

The consistencies are simple and basic. I viewed each of my bosses as if he were a high school principal. (And in my time, pre-student strikes and riots, a principal was the quintessence of unimpeachable power and an unquestionable figure of respect.) While I harbored deep-down hopes of moving on to executive levels myself, I served in each job as if it were my pot at the end of the rainbow. At the same time I was aware that some day this man I was serving would be called upon to give me a promotion or, if I moved on, a recommendation. His response would surely be based upon a cumulative impression of me and my work, not a last-minute surge of best-behavior productiveness at the eleventh hour.

Four of my ex-bosses can best be described as father figures. They worried about my health, inquired about my social life, tempered their requests or assignments with kindliness and affection. I don't think I betrayed their concern and consideration. I don't believe I consciously took advantage of their protectiveness. But I do remember feeling quite safe and cozy working for these four men. My tenures with each of them were marked with warm feelings of being appreciated as some kind of child prodigy. My departures from them were distinguished by the truly unselfish send-off each gave me and the hearty good wishes which went with me as I moved on to greener pastures. I have remained good friends with each. In the eight or ten years since I worked for them I have met these four men sometimes on an equal, or almost equal, professional footing or I have called upon them on many occasions for advice and for favors, and I have never been given a short answer.

Father figures make great bosses and if they are in their fifties or sixties, happily married and content in their work, they make great friends. I recommend them highly.

Pals make nice bosses too. I had three of this kind. Each of these men was younger than my father-figure bosses and I was further along in my career when I worked in each of those three jobs. Bosses who are pals are more interested in your political opinions than in your health. They are more apt to introduce you to their bachelor friends than to inquire solicitously about your social life. They are more natural and instinctual in their dealings with you, substituting the familiarity of contemporaries for the protectiveness of the daddy-type boss. Pal bosses who are secure in their own jobs are most likely to give you a professional boost. They like to see a buddy make out well.

One of my bosses was of the old school. If this man were to have a sampler hanging on his wall, it would read, "The business of business is business." In fact, this guy was an inveterate maxim coiner. Some of his favorites were: Shut Up and Put Out, or Ours Is Not to Shirk—Ours Is But to Work, or Familiarity Breeds High Rent. (This last one, I finally figured out, is based on the precept that output produces profits which offset the rent for office space and, conversely, chummy conversations are time-wasting, nonproductive and thus uneconomical, rent-wise.)

You get the general idea. This category of nose-to-the-grindstone boss is a fading breed. But if you've drawn one in the job lottery you know that he is easy to work for if you're a hard worker and hard to work for if you're easygoing. My grindstone boss insisted on being called Mister. He didn't stand on every ceremony in the book but I just *knew* that he appreciated a "Yes, sir" or a "No, sir" every now and then. He was most pleased with neatness, accuracy and a willingness to stay after hours if the work load required it. He was not especially thrilled with spurts of *creative* effort from his secretary/assistant. As soon as I accepted the fact that the office was not to be an extension of Fun City, I was quite able to enjoy this job and to concentrate on the serious business of business. I may not be as crazy about this boss as the others in retrospect, but I learned a hell of a lot standing at the grindstone along with him.

A close relative of this type of boss is the misogynist. You may meet him as a boss in your climbing years or as colleague later on. In either incarnation he's easily recognizable by his unmistakable disregard for women. All women, usually. But women in business, always and without fail.

When this misogynist character is your boss he can mask his mindless hatred of women beneath a façade. He can simply be known as a tough, demanding taskmaster very much like the boss I just described. He may accord you the human recognition he gives to a passing window washer. And you will probably attribute his attitude to the fact that you are just a lowly secretary.

But the real clue to his hang-up is the fact that he treats the female vice president of the company the same way. This type of guy doesn't reform just because he's dealing with a woman of rank. It's wise to recognize a misogynist at first glance. Once the source of his problem is clear to you, his behavior shouldn't be your problem. When you find yourself on an equal plane with a misogynist, don't expect any miracles. No matter how brilliantly you perform, he will never be persuaded of your worth. Stated most simply, he can't deal with women, he can't believe a woman could possibly be capable and he can't accept the fact that anyone in the company is taking you seriously. *He* certainly won't be fooled.

The best course of action to follow if a misogynist is unavoidable, either as a colleague or a boss, is be respectful, formal, perfect at your job and alert for a way out of his department.

Before getting to the last of my male bosses I have to add a few words of wisdom about a type of boss that I never experienced firsthand—the romantic interest or the flirt. I've had to depend on friends for on-the-scene live coverage. The reports are somewhat conflicting. While most informants describe their bosses who are love interests just the way the novels do, some girls swear that the relationship needs a more refined definition —that it can go a step beyond palship and a step short of romantic involvement.

Variations on a theme

One girl who has had fantastic success on this narrow precipice doesn't have to take a blood oath. I would never in a million years believe that she and her boss had an affair because the boss is such an innocent, naïve and pure little lamb. He is married to an angelic woman, has four darling kids and is clearly Father-of-the-Year material. As for the assistant, she had a thriving out-of-the-office romance in progress. Still, the girl and her boss did have a strange thing going. They seemed to exist during the day only to please each other. She worried his worries for him. She cushioned bad blows. She praised, she admired, she worshiped his every line of dictation. He, in turn, complimented her on her clothes and her file drawers with equal sincerity. He bought her all nine Beethoven symphonies recorded by Toscanini when she mentioned that she loved the Eroica. He seemed to get raises for her when all the other departments in the company were pulling in the belts on their budgets.

This mutual-devotion society of theirs defies explanation. All I can tell you is that the last Grand Gesture really takes the seven-layer cake. The boss arranged for the girl to have a parking space in the executive parking lot with her own name stenciled onto the asphalt. And if you know Thing One about status symbols in Big Biz you can just imagine how this development made eyes roll and tongues wag.

But these two are as much beyond human understanding as they are beyond suspicion. So go figure it. Or maybe it's simply a situation where two plain, nice people who like and respect each other, enjoy working together and gain pleasure out of making each other happy. If so, hear! hear!

Most of the girls who volunteered information about the love-interest-type boss gave more coventional descriptions of the lay of the land. Flirting was a common denominator. Dressing provocatively was an often admitted sin. Dating was common —with varying testimony about how this did or did not affect the effectiveness of the working relationship. Full-fledged affairs were rare, and in most cases girls told me that they didn't but they knew someone who did. . . .

More about that in the next chapter.

As I've said before, the dream about marrying the boss is nine parts myth and one part wishful thinking. Bosses, for the most part, are aware of the hazards of playing around in their own backyards. Since most companies frown upon intramural liaisons, a man has too much riding on his career to risk it all on a cute chick no matter how accessible she may be and no matter how unmarried he may be. This fact, plus the realization that in nine bosses I had not one romantic-interest type (a statistical oddity if they *are* common) plus the results of my once-over-lightly research, lead me to the inescapable conclusion that the boss as a love figure is a phenomenon which exists more often in the eye of the beholder than in real life.

Fortunately for me, my last boss is my present boss. He runs what most employers would call a loose ship, to say the least. But he seems to get more work per hour out of his staff than a galley full of slave drivers could. With fairly frequent bursts of generosity beyond the call of duty and a general attitude of consideration for an employee's private concerns, any boss can alter his image and his office's atmosphere. Challenge your boss one of these days. Reassure him that the concept of the following innovations and celebrations is more awesome than the practical reality of them:

The better bosses' manual

(1) Take your employees out for a celebration lunch at a top restaurant on each annual anniversary of the day they started to work for the company.

(2) A birthday bonus wouldn't kill you, would it?

(3) When the company makes a smashing profit, share it with your minions—even if you have no formal profit-sharing program. It's a simple matter of drawing a few extra checks for the people who really deserve the rewards.

(4) Throw a fun party (we're partial to champagne in our office) for an hour or less at the drop of a piece of good news or the landing of a big client. Surely, there must be something to celebrate besides Christmas.

(5) If an employee is knocking herself out in a two-hour commute from a remote suburban cul-de-sac, try a little tenderness, understanding and monetary aid to lighten her burden. Tell her to give up the bus-train-taxi route and to drive her car into town instead. When you pick up her parking fees each month you'll feel like Sir Lancelot and Santa Claus rolled up into one.

(6) Adjust to the unexpected. Don't react to once-in-a-lifetime events with traditional rules and regulations. If the astronauts parade through your city, give the girls the morning off. When the power fails in your building and your secretary is stuck in a stalled elevator from 5:30 to 7 P.M.—on her own time—send her a transistor radio with a card, "More power to you." She'll never forget you for it. If her parents pop in from Grand Rapids let her go home early to clean up her apartment and shop for dinner.

On one of those once-in-a-lifetime crisis crazy days my boss really came through. My baby-sitter had called in sick at 8 A.M. and I had to set up a news conference that day. With Mr. Geis's permission I lugged my little girls to the office and hoped for a miracle to get through the day. My boss saw the state I was in and assigned his secretary to feed, amuse and distract the twins all day long while my staff and I handled the phone calls and telegrams for a solid eight hours.

I was awed by my boss's generous attitude. But as he pointed out, this press conference wasn't a self-indulgence. It was a function of the job I was doing for him and his author. On that particular day it was the most important thing going on in our office and worth contributing his secretary's services for the cause.

My daughters enjoyed every minute of their office adventure. They thrived on the attention of a new person, they were enchanted by the water cooler, they typed the print off two typewriters, they made magnificent paper-clip necklaces *and* they learned a little bit about what their mother does and where she does it. From that time on, my children speak of my office with the same familiarity that they assign to the homes of their aunts and uncles.

I don't suggest that twenty-seven million women bring their children to work. But I do suggest that unusual problems demand unusual solutions.

(7) A little bonus for an employee's marriage or new baby wouldn't hurt much, or a going-away present, or a tiny trinket for the girl who comes in on Saturday. (Even though she gets overtime, it's the extras that are appreciated.)

(8) Employees aren't furniture. Don't pass a girl's desk with a visitor without introducing them to one another by name. It's a small courtesy that requires even smaller effort. But if the visitor is famous or handsome or fascinating, the introduction could make a girl's day.

Whenever one of the newspaper or magazine reporters comes to interview my boss, he never fails to bring the man around to my office and to the offices of our top editors. And he doesn't just introduce us. He times a plug with each handshake. He might announce, "Letty is the girl responsible for all those promotions you were just admiring," or "If it weren't for Don we never could have signed our hottest new author" or "Our last book that hit the best-seller list was edited by Jackie." It does wonders for our egos and sometimes it gets our names in print as well.

(9) Give raises without waiting to be asked. Keep a note on your calendar pad to remind you when it's been six months or a year since your employee's last raise. If she's deserving, let her know that an increase is on its way. Or let her at least be aware that you're aware that a raise is due. Even if you can't swing it with the exchequer at this time, a girl appreciates

knowing that you recognize her good performance and you are batting for her.

(10) Practice the same brand of loyalty as you expect from your employees. Don't assume the worst when you hear an accusation. Don't fire on hearsay. Don't cry "embezzlement" without first asking questions. Your secretary may have used the petty cash to buy your wife the birthday present you clean forgot.

This decalogue of perfect boss behavior doesn't fit every situation. Obviously, it wouldn't be practicable in an enormous organization or in a company where the purse strings are tied to the buttons of a computer. But your boss should get the general idea. There are ways of keeping a working relationship cold and briskly formal. And there are ways of humanizing it.

In our shop there are dozens of humanizing examples to cite. We receive suggestions not commandments; we are consulted as to our own tastes when our offices are being redesigned; our advice is sought on all major publishing decisions; we are encouraged to bring our work out to the terrace on top of our building on warm sunny days; we have free access to the boss's liquor cabinet; we don't answer for our comings and goings, within reason; we encounter no pettiness about petty cash; we watch television for astronaut take-offs, splash-downs, moratoriums, world series clinchers, election results and presidential addresses; we are trusted and respected. Of course, this is practicable for our staff of twenty whereas it would be unmanageable for two thousand. But you can do things like that on a limited departmental scale, I'm sure.

It seems so simple. And our boss reports that it is.

Colleagues and coworkers

Picture this sticky wicket: Rachel and Ralph hold identical jobs as associate editors at a major magazine. Each is responsible for an equal number of publishing houses and literary agents. Each is expected to scout both sources for possible magazine articles which can be excerpted from books or to turn up talented authors to write original stories for the magazine. Rachel and Ralph occupy private offices of approximately the same dimensions. They have comparable expense accounts. They've been employed at the magazine for precisely the same number of years. Each is earning $12,000 a year.

Rachel thinks Ralph is peachy keen. Ralph thinks Rachel is hunky dory. Everything is copacetic—until their superior leaves the company. There follows an executive upheaval of the first water. Solid ground becomes quicksand and security turns into mutual suspicion. When the tide subsides who's going to come out on top? That decision is in top-managment's hands and where Ralph and Rachel are concerned it's a tough one.

The management committee decided to interview both of them. Given their similar records of high performance and long employment, the committee hoped that the personal factor would help them determine which, if either, should be raised to the top editor's position.

Ralph took the more hostile tack. He was smart enough to realize that an outright attack on his colleague would be a transparent bid for power. Besides, his long-standing fondness for Rachel really did not allow him to take the offensive so unfeelingly. So he zeroed in on what he felt was a "fair" criticism of Rachel: she might get married and leave the company.

During his interview he responded to all questions about himself with honesty and good sense. When asked whether he thought Rachel might make a good editor he said she'd be super. But he added: "Of course, with young women in their twenties one is always taking a chance that they may abandon their careers for marriage or motherhood. As between the two of us, I frankly feel that I'm a safer gamble for you because my career is more important to me."

Rachel had a strong reserve of good feelings for Ralph, too. But she followed through on them with honor and constancy and her responses during her interview were based on that honor as well as on good sense. She wanted the bigger job as dearly as Ralph did and she deserved it just as much. However, friendship meant as much to her as advancement and in this instance she realized that the fruits of success might be bitter. She told the committee: "Ralph and I have been working as a team for so long now that I don't feel either of us would be able to adjust to the other becoming captain at this point. May I suggest that you consider a dual promotion with perhaps a modified salary raise for each of us? We could dispense with the middle editor's position entirely. Ralph and I would handle all the work of the department and we would be directly responsible to the editor in chief. In that way, neither of us would be competing with the other, both of us would enjoy a promotion and both of us would feel comfortable about staying on."

As you may have guessed, the committee bought Rachel's recommendation top to bottom. After splitting the former editor's salary between Ralph and Rachel, two major positions were created and the company payroll was not increased. Between them, Ralph and Rachel handled the expanded work load with no strain. Their friendship was intact and the department was streamlined in the process.

While Ralph was not behaving despicably in citing Rachel's

marriageability, Rachel was obviously the more loyal colleague.
Ralph's reaction was indeed a human one: to get what he could
for himself. Admittedly he was not cruel or derisive in going
about it. His only claim to superiority was that he was a man.
Nevertheless, Rachel is our idealized case in point.

A job is never so precious as a human being and his feelings.
A friendship cannot be bought with a raise in salary. Ambition
at the expense of others is craven aggressiveness.

You may get the squeeze in big-power plays or small ones
like the one attempted against Rachel. But you are not likely to
be thoroughly victimized. Take comfort in the fact that very
often your fate and your colleague's are often in other hands.
Even in the Ralph and Rachel example, it was not a one-to-one
tension. They were not alone in the arena. They were playing
off the management committee. The committee recognized
Ralph's blitz attempt for what it was. They understood his motives and did not overly condemn them. However, in this case
the company could operate from its own knowledge and experience. They still clung to the practice of *hiring* a man rather
than a woman on the grounds of possible marriage dropout. But
they had discovered that once an unmarried girl has racked up
career time exceeding five years, she is almost as unlikely to
abandon her job for *anything* as a man is. Companies are on to
this interesting fact, and so the male-superiority gap is narrowing
even more. Men and women who are equals in job responsibility
can thus compete with complete fairness on performance and
record alone.

With male coworkers an added dimension of fun comes into
play at meetings and in daily consultations. Even without any
flirting or romantic interest it is more exciting for a woman to
be dealing on the same level as a man. It is pleasing to the ego
to be called into meetings and to find that you are the only
woman. It is nice to know that a male feels comfortable dis-

cussing mutual business concerns with you—even though you
know that you just finished such purely feminine activities as
polishing your nails or planning your dinner menu. While you
are enjoying being the only girl in the board room, don't forget
that our aim is to get more women into the inner sanctum.
Don't expect to be the only one forever.

I get a great charge out of really serious business discussions
with men. Sometimes I find that I am standing outside myself
watching myself make official-looking notes on a project or
hearing myself talk with passionate concern about profit and
loss statements or point-of-sale display material. Is this the same
me who giggles at my children's riddles? Is this the same voice
that argues with the supermarket manager about a mismarked
can of peas? It *is* the same me *and* a different me, both of which
coexist within the same body and, as I fondly believe, make
for a better, total person.

If you think about it, the difference between objecting to an
overpriced can of peas and objecting to an overpriced advertising invoice is not so enormous as it may seem. Both require an
exercise of judgment, a capacity to be outraged for the right
reasons and the confidence to speak up for one's opinions. If
you can manage to cope with your dry cleaner or your landlord,
there's a better chance that you can handle yourself just fine
with all the men that office life sends in your direction. And
vice versa.

Being a Miss or a Mrs. among Misters should be a constant
source of pleasure for you. If you like what you do, if you don't
feel threatened by some grasping hotshot, if you are consulted,
complimented and compensated, you should be sitting pretty.
Hang-ups about femininity should melt away. Worries about
being accepted as a thinking individual should disappear. The
need to prove yourself should be nonexistent. You should be at
peace in a land of plenty. With your business life in such good

shape you should be able to devote all your energies to your personal life. And that's not my business.

Did I hear a moan?

You mean this idyllic picture doesn't quite match up with your own situation?

If not, then I'll bet the fatal flaw is spelled S-E-X. Not the passionate lights-out kind. But the S factor in your relationships with your colleagues. Ask yourself these questions: Are you being unconsciously seductive? (Or consciously) Are you wearing inappropriate, revealing clothes to the office? If so, you must realize that they make men more uncomfortable than excited. You don't have to dress like Melina Mercouri to remind the men you work with that you're a girl. It's nigh onto impossible for a bunch of gray flannel executives to talk about sales figures if *your* figure is flashing sex signals across the room. You may get some appreciative stares and a wink or two. But in the long run you'll defeat your purpose. Your male colleague will feel guilty about his interest in your pulchritude. He'll be distracted from the business at hand. A funny reaction may set in. His mind will wander; he won't listen. He may feel that a woman he thinks about going to bed with is not one to give the responsibility of taming a tough client or landing a major account. Try this unspoken resolution with the next male colleague you meet: "I'm going to be attractive, but you won't mind. You'll notice me but I won't make you squirm, I promise."

It's important to be a woman first and a woman executive second. It's important for *you*. But if you come on as Female Incarnate to your colleagues you'll start men beating their chests and bellowing, "Me, Tarzan; You, Jane" when they should be saying something like "Me, Artist; You, Copywriter."

There's more in the quiz if all is not well in your coed executive locker room. Are you wise to the menace of meetings, for example?

Meetings bring out the dame in some damsels. The most charming, diplomatic ladies are often turned into harping, pushy clubwomen at the close of the board room door. There's something about a table with chairs arranged around it that arouses the coffee-klatch mentality into action. So test yourself.

Do you rush to the head of the table or to the front of the room? Are you always beelining it to the president's side? If so, you're committing the sin of the obvious. Don't you realize that it is more sensible to sit in the least important position at the conference table? People will have to turn to see you. They will notice you quite enough because you are a woman. Some men may feel threatened by that fact alone. You needn't ram it down their throats by rushing to the front of the class. You will make your points by what you contribute, not by your conception of a status-seating plan.

Do you participate too much? Do you feel you have to come up with one idea after another in order to justify your presence? Again, ridiculous reasoning. By calling such annoying attention to yourself you run the risk of saying five dumb things for every brilliant one. You also reaffirm the old platitudes about women who can't keep their mouths shut. You strike some men as too eager. You interrupt the flow of the meeting. You logjam the agenda. You accomplish nothing except perhaps to inspire a motion to ban girls from the board room.

If you have something worthwhile to contribute, do you shriek, shout, rasp, interrupt or whine? A well-modulated, controlled voice radiates authority. It breeds confidence in the listener. In fact, you might try an experiment to prove the point to yourself. At your next conference, speak so softly that men will have to strain to hear you. You'll be amazed at how hard they'll listen.

I should add here that I'm a poor student of my own teachings. My voice is always climbing to high registers that would make a chorus of *castrati* envious. If I'm jubilant, I shout. If something is very funny, I roar. If I'm angry, I explode. But I'm improving. Eavesdrop on my tone of voice when I'm arguing for more advertising money or pitching an author as a guest on a television show and I'd rival any graduate of the Dale Carnegie course. So there's hope for all of us.

Are you stubborn? Do you stick by your opinion so rigidly that people want to tell you where to stick it? Try listening—but really listening—to the next guy. Give him recognition for good points along the way even if you disagree with his overall theory. If you're always busy making men notice how smart you are, two nasty things can happen: they can be hurt by the knowledge that it's true—and nobody likes to have his inferiority advertised at a meeting of his fellows; or they can resent your pontification so thoroughly that they will be in no frame of mind to appreciate the real merits of your opinions.

My friend, the girl computer wizard, told me about a trick she uses to sway an opponent at a conference. "If a man disagrees with me I ask him to verbalize *my* point of view for the edification of everyone. When he does so, in his own words, he is not only more apt to understand what I've been driving at, but he is proud of his comprehension. It works miracles. Before anyone knows it, he's arguing my side of the case." Clever, these computer people.

Outside contacts, clients or customers

From subordinate mailboys, bosses and male coworkers it's an easy step to manhandling the guys in the great outside. There's one big difference. The contact is occasional, not every day. The impression you make is a one-shot thing or a four-times-a-year ritual. Rather than being ships that pass in the night, you and these occasional male contacts are gradually building a sort of totem-pole image of each other. Each time you meet another impression is added—like one colorful figure standing on the shoulders of the one beneath him. Whether you are lunch-date friends, which we've already discussed at length, or telephone pals or long-distance buddies (kind of like having a man in every port), this category of mankind adds to the fun, frolic and variety of your professional tasks.

I have dozens of pals whom I've never seen and will probably never meet. We have been on a first-name basis for years. We write to each other about book business matters and we write to each other to announce a baby's birth or a killing on the stock market. We exchange Christmas cards and sometimes gifts. I know their voices as well as I know the color of my best friend's eyes.

These are my long-distance friends. The office telephone and the company stationery have made us pals over the years. They hail from as far as Melbourne, Australia, and Capetown, South Africa, and as near as two blocks away in Manhattan. I call a man my long-distance friend if the nature of our business dealings demands no personal contact. In my profession, he may be a bookseller in Colorado to whom I write about window-display contests. He may be a newscaster in New Orleans who is producing a special on "What Makes a Best Seller." He may be a newspaper columnist in Philadelphia with whom I set up an author interview. Or he may be a literary agent in Tokyo who represents our books in arranging for Japanese translations.

Once the business is taken up and laid aside there are always a few moments to make contact. Real human contact that counts toward making the two of us flesh and blood people and not just names in a file folder. The New Orleans man and I have argued about integration. With the Colorado man I've explored air pollution. With the Philadelphia columnist I've sweated out his pains at being widowed and his joy at remarrying. These faraway friends know my children's names and I know their opinions on American foreign policy. They look up college friends for me and they make vacation recommendations or even hotel reservations for us.

Your job may not involve such far-flung business relationships. But I'll wager that you can name six people you've spoken to during the past month whom you must deal with only infrequently and whom you have no real reason or likelihood to meet. If they're in another city or country you're missing a nice business bonus if you don't give a little extra to the conversation or add a personal note to your letters. If they're close at hand you might consider having a "no reason" lunch with someone to whom you've been directing purchase orders for a year and a half.

I'm afraid that the business world suffers from too many order-and-fulfillment relationships where only the necessary information is communicated and people continue signing their mail "Yours very sincerely" after twenty years of corresponding.

To combat this you might try "Cordially" at first. Then work up to "All the best" or "As ever" or even "Cheers." Anything that lightens the load of a business communication keeps the human element alive and is good for us all. I adore people who say what they have to say and then close their letters or phone calls with an anecdote or even just an amusing word about something in the news. A long-distance pal of mine writes the most poetic final paragraphs about the effect of the seasons on the foliage around his English farmhouse. A Spanish correspondent knows I'm a cooking fiend and every few letters he throws in one of his wife's best recipes. A Detroit telephone friend gave me an astonishing firsthand report of that city's riots. You see, you might even learn something!

And don't feel guilty about wasting the company's writing paper or beefing up its phone bills. Nobody's suggesting that you spend an hour on aimless chitchat. But a few extra personal words can make friends for the company faster than three public relations experts hired for the purpose. Most companies are enlightened enough to allow you to cultivate faraway friends wherever they may be. So put your feet up and dictate something chummy to that actuary in Des Moines. You'll make his day.

I owe to my job one of the most fantastic pen pals any girl can boast. Groucho Marx. Groucho's epistles are so legendary that they were the material for an entire book, *The Groucho Letters,* which was greeted with glee by every lover of wit and humor.

Because my company published two of his other books, I was lucky enough to work with Groucho to help publicize them—which, quite honestly, wasn't *work* at all. When the great mustache wasn't in New York I manufactured reasons to write to him in Hollywood just to guarantee myself a letter from him in return. Imagine finding a few of these specimens in your "In" Box:

Dear Letty,
Next Saturday night on ABC, you can see me cavorting on a show called "The Hollywood Palace." Out here it's known as the Ed Sullivan Show *sans* Ed Sullivan. I think you'll enjoy it. Among other things, it includes an elephant named Bertha. At the end of the show I ride off on this pachyderm to hysterical applause. A fine finish for a man who should be living quietly in some senior citizen's city!

I would write more but I'm busy rehearsing for a show I'm doing for Chrysler. This may be the greatest thing that's ever happened to General Motors.

My best to the shadowy Mr. Geis and his family, and love to you and that labor leader.

Fondly,
Groucho

Dear Letty,

If America ever has a female President, I'm sure you'll get the job.

Now that you've hooked Mr. Pogrebin you're beginning to feel your oats—unless that's Mr. Pogrebin's pleasure. For all I know, he may be a professional oat-feeler who was born on a farm where the only method of evacuation was an oat house. (This, as I told that character from Saturday Review who you maneuvered into nailing me on the phone, is an example of the lowest form of humor.)

There was also a ballplayer with the New York Giants whose name, believe it or not, was Mel Ott. Many people, not knowing what they were doing, used to take great pains to explain that he was an "ottfielder."

A morning TV show called "Your First Impression," which is precisely the same as 38 others which are seen from nine to noon each day, has offered me no money but has given me the choice between a refrigerator and a set of tires. This is certainly a hell of a choice. If I take the icebox I'll be unable to drive to the Springs. If I take the tires I'll have no place to put the cottage cheese and those halves of apples that some louse here at home keeps caching away in the refrigerator.

Love,
Groucho

Dear Letty,

Having just finished the old year, I guess we should all be grateful that except for a few major wars around the world, most of us are still in one piece.

Speaking of one piece (which is about all I had in 1964), where the hell is the baby?"

Love,
Groucho

This is a small sampling of the correspondence I've enjoyed with Groucho. From a matter-of-fact report of publicity activities our letters progressed to become fond exchanges of news and views. I value them with great affection.

Traveling salesmen and passing strangers

If you can manage to locate, develop and nurture that elusive best self that we mentioned earlier, you'll be operating at full-personality tilt no matter what stripe of man comes your way. You won't have to switch gears either if a guy materializes in your professional orbit and you find that he defies definition. This can be anyone from a traveling salesman of the old school to a hotel banquet manager whom you may meet while *you're* traveling.

The secure, confident lady executive who has really found herself will have a personal style, a public image which remain steadfast no matter where she is and whom she meets. She will be as comfortable with a messenger boy as she is with a bank president. She will be as at ease in a café in Istanbul as she is in the corner Nedick's. She will be as interested and attentive to the space salesman she has been trying to avoid as she is to her own boss.

One would think that this kind of counsel was so obvious as to require no comment. And yet, with all the "Do Unto Other" reminders in the world, you can still see girls saving their best personalities for their boy friends, bosses and best clients. Playing Jekyll and Hyde is not only unhealthy (like going from the hot sun into an ice bath), it's bad business. That funny-looking unemployed actor that you brush off today could become Academy Award-winning Michael J. Pollard tomorrow. That old man you haughtily questioned in the reception room might turn out to be the boss's grandfather. That overeager college kid who pursued you for an interview for his school paper could end up a

Pulitzer Prize reporter in three years—and wouldn't you love to have him owe you a favor then?

Even if good behavior doesn't pay off in the long run, it pays off in the short haul. It makes you feel better about yourself. Passing strangers and traveling salesmen have wives and children and secret tragedies and as many sensitive feelings as you do. Just because they may be scratching their way up in some niche of the business world that you don't think much of doesn't mean that they've developed a callus in the place of a heart. Though your cold and rational business self knows that you would probably never buy fabric from Sam Smith, let your best self overrule. Give Sammy five minutes of your time. He's only trying to make a living.

Married men and men for married women

There's a book around with the intriguing title *Married Men Make the Best Lovers*. If you have the kind of experience that leads you to agree with that sentiment, then tune out here and now. You'll find me hopelessly square on this subject and emphatically sure I'm right, too.

Married men make the best business associates in my opinion. As a wife and mother of three (my son was born sometime between the writing of Chapter 5 and Chapter 6 of this book), I have a lot in common with married men. My husband is one.

I'm a lot more conversant with joint returns than is a single girl. If I can't talk about playing squash from personal experience, I can talk about my husband's game with great authority. I can directly sympathize with tight mortgage money, a man's view of childbirth, and the high cost of Brooks Brothers suits. Living with a man in a close and intimate marriage prepares a girl well for relaxed conversation with other married men. We all know that business isn't always strictly business. But it doesn't have to be monkey business either.

Any man I meet more than once knows a little something about my husband. Single men know about him because it is often necessary to establish that the gold band on my finger stands for something more than a bill from Tiffany's. Married men know about him because I cite him as my source of information on most subjects outside of publishing. Everyone who knows about him knows I adore him. I believe that it's close to impossible to make a pass at a woman who loves her husband as vociferously as I do.

But the making of passes isn't the most common trait of married businessmen—despite what foreign movies would lead us to believe. Most often, getting along with married businessmen is like getting along with businessmen, period. If you are single and you have *his* marriage on your mind, that's your problem.

You'll have to examine your reactions. A friend of mine feels unattractive and unfeminine if men, both married and single, don't lech after her. Another girl is wary of married men on the make and uncomfortable with married men who are contented husbands. She doesn't know how to parry the advances of the first type or to warm to the casual conversation of the second. Neither a bore nor a whore must you be, I remind her in a clumsy paraphrase from *Hamlet*. But I suspect she won't know how to cool it without being cold until she's a married woman herself.

Men for Married Women may have struck you as a moral contradiction when you noticed the last subheading above. But once I explain, you'll see why I have a special warm spot in my heart for this category. Though the names have been changed, here's my own real-life honor roll of men met in the line of duty who, for one reason or another, make perfect men friends for a

married woman: Alex, an author's attorney, who hands out my
husband's business cards to those of his clients who need a labor
lawyer; Mel, the television producer, who invited my husband
to our dinner meeting so that he could interview me as long as
was necessary, and has ended up a friend of the family; Henry,
head of an advertising agency with theatrical accounts, who is
always pressing free movie tickets upon us; Stan, the free-lance
publicist—he liked me so much, he wanted his wife to meet me;
I liked him so much I wanted my husband to meet him; all
four of us have been buddies for nearly five years.

Men for Married Women are businessmen who don't always
call meetings for five-thirty when you have to have dinner on the
table at home by six o'clock. They are bosses who ask you to
bring your husband to the weekend convention in Washington.
(Why should you two spend the weekend apart? How much
more could a double room be? Your husband would be delighted
to tour the national monuments while you make the rounds of
convention booths, wouldn't he?) Men for Married Women are
business friends who realize that there's a wife and mother
behind that efficient career-girl façade. They make a lady executive's husband rejoice in her job, not resent it. They make a
pregnant woman feel that it's perfectly all right to wear maternity clothes and support stockings to the office or to make four-
teen visits to the ladies' room between lunch and closing time.

No rules of manhandling are required for these princes. In
reality, *they're* handling *us*—with kid gloves and great understanding. All we have to do is appreciate them.

Taking advantage of your advantages

You single working girls may not get the nuances of the
foregoing discussion. But you will nod in unison when I state
unequivocally that there are times when your job should serve

you as loyally as you serve it. In other words, while some misguided girls use sex to get a job, very few seem to use their job to get some sex or, rather, a member of the opposite sex. (I am definitely *not* talking about husband hunting on the office premises.)

I already divulged the subterfuge I used when I first met my husband. I confided to him a knotty copyright problem, gave him my card and asked him to call me at the office with some legal advice. Of course, my company retains legal counsel for just such consulting services. But my husband-to-be didn't know that. He might have suspected it. But he didn't know it for sure. Very gracefully he went along with the fiction that I needed *his* legal advice. He called me four days later, we were engaged twelve weeks later and married three months after that. We still get a large laugh about the effectiveness of my put-on. And with all his teasing, I'm not sure whether or not he really knew what I was up to all along.

Husbands I can't guarantee. But I can give firsthand assurances that this harmless little ploy can yield great dates for the duration of your singlehood. It makes every day Sadie Hawkins Day. Never again need you be at the mercy of a man's whim to talk or not to talk to you. Armed with only such vital statistics as his occupation and marital status, you can take the conversational initiative without sacrificing a wisp of femininity —*if* you make your job do the work of breaking the ice for you. The gambit only works if there is a logical and believable reason for you to open a conversation. *Example:* At a crowded party some years ago I saw a magnificent-looking man whom I was dying to meet. He was surrounded by women throughout the evening. He was there stag. I knew that I would never see him again if we didn't meet then and there. He was a six-foot-two version of Paul Newman and I'm a Newman fan from way back. I just had to make a move.

By eavesdropping on his conversation with a gaggle of adoring girls I learned that he was an independent filmmaker. On his next trip to replenish his drink at the bar, I intercepted.

"Did I hear you talking a minute ago about wanting to make documentary shorts?" I asked in my best professional manner.

"That's right," he said. "We've been doing industrial films for so long I'm beginning to feel stale."

"Well, I might have something for you if you're in the mood for social significance." I lured him into a corner of the room with his fresh drink in hand and for one hour we talked about a book that had just been published by my company and that I felt had great film potential.

I knew damn well that no independent filmmaker could afford to buy the rights to this book. But I wasn't promising to sign any contracts, was I? Well, one thing led to another and at the end of the hour we decided to continue our discussion over dinner.

That this Paul Newman look-alike turned out to be a narcissistic bore is not the point. I would never have known whether he was great or godawful if I hadn't met him, and I would never have met him without the all-powerful social crutch of my job. Sometimes the gambit yields a loser and sometimes a winner. But you can't say much more for a blind date or a church supper either.

A goody-goody friend of mine decries the "dishonesty" in this little exercise. That's as absurd as claiming that wearing powder and lipstick is compromising your "honest" skin tones. There's a little bit of gamesmanship in every courtship situation. Once a meaningful relationship is under way, straightshooting is in order. But for openers, almost anything goes. To my way of thinking, as long as I give my all to a job, I have every right to use my job for whatever little marginal advantages it can offer me.

And my husband agrees with me.

6.

The helping hand and how to keep it off your body

*O*ne basic commandment will stand you in good stead in matters of sex in the business world, so commit it to memory: *Expect the Unexpected.*

Take my little go-around with Brendan Behan. I've told you about Behan, the dear, devilish Irish playwright-author whom I shepherded around New York. And I told you how I adored him and how amusing he was. But it wasn't always so. In fact, the very first night that I met Brendan Behan was nearly a disaster of the first order.

It all began one morning in Dublin when Brendan went out for a pack of cigarettes. When he hadn't returned seven hours later, his wife Beatrice wasn't too surprised to receive a phone call from Brendan in New York City. He just felt like a visit to godless Gotham and so he caught a plane and came. Bernard Geis was no less surprised to hear Brendan's Irish brogue on the other end of the telephone that same fine Sunday morning. Brendan said he had come to New York to work. Since our company had him under a three-book contract this announcement was good news indeed. Mr. and Mrs. Geis were happy to accept when Brendan invited himself to their apartment presumably for a social visit. It wasn't until much later that the real reason for Brendan's impassioned visit dawned on the

Geises: on Sunday the public bars in New York don't open until noon. He made several heart-rending pleas for a "snort." But the Geises were not about to float an alcoholic down the drain. Finally Brendan checked a clock, saw that it was five minutes of twelve and beat a hasty farewell to catch the nearest bartender for his first pour of the day.

We didn't hear from him for a week. Rather than consider the Behan contracts moribund, Mr. Geis decided to take action.

"Find Brendan and see if you can get him writing," he said to me one morning.

Though far removed from my publicity, promotion or advertising responsibilities, this had to be the most challenging assignment of my career. I took to it with great gusto. A few well-placed calls to various police precincts and midtown pubs established without doubt that Brendan was very much off the wagon. I left the same message for Brendan with bartenders and drinking buddies around the city—"Meet Letty at a midnight-to-dawn party in Greenwich Village tonight." I'll never know how many passing strangers picked up that invitation and the accompanying address because the party was a mob scene to begin with. But the message did reach Mr. Behan and that was what mattered most. He showed up at the party at three o'clock in the morning wearing leather shoes with no socks, a rope for a belt and singing an unprintable verse of "Roll Me Over." He was loaded but he was there.

I introduced myself as the Letty of the message. I presented my credentials as Bernard Geis's minion. I told him that I had invited him to this party which was being given by some of my friends, just so that I could locate him and get him onto a disciplined writing schedule. I reminded him of his contractual obligations. I assured him that I had used this party as a ruse to track him down and that his drinking and roistering days were over.

"Damned clever, these New York girls," he said with a crooked smile as a bespectacled young man led him away to a group of young literati eager to worship Behan's arrival as the Second Coming of Dylan Thomas.

Two hours later I had him in a cab and finally we reached his hotel—a disreputable-looking hostelry in the Times Square area. Brendan promised he would come to my office at ten o'clock the next morning ready to start work. I was congratulating myself for a job well done as I bade him goodnight in the hotel lobby and started out the door. Brendan was plastered. He was probably the drunkest man I had ever seen, before or since. I would not have believed him strong enough for the scene that followed.

"And where the hell do ya think yer goin', Missy?" he shouted. The desk clerk looked up. I stopped in my tracks, one hand on the revolving door. "If you take one more step out of this place I'll send this fucking ashtray out of that pretty plate-glass window."

He was brandishing a heavy, brass, free-standing ashtray. Holding it like a baseball bat, he directed his gaze right at the hotel's front window.

"You'd better come up to me room because if you don't, I'll rip this place apart. Then Bearney (Berney always came out Bearney in Brendan's speech) Geis'll have quite a lot of ex-plainin' to do. Just wait 'til the New York *Times* starts askin' of him what his star author and his publicity girl were doin' cuttin' up a hotel lobby at five o'clock in the mornin'."

I thought for a moment about that. Still frozen to the floor right next to the exit I reasoned the whole thing out. I was single then, nobody was waiting up for me, no one even knew where I was. Brendan was certainly rambunctious but he was too drunk to do me any harm. If he started wrecking the hotel, the police would come, the hotel would sue and the newspapers would get the story. It was not the type of publicity that I am supposed to achieve for our company.

I turned around, took Brendan's arm, relieved him of his ashtray and walked with him into the elevator.

His room was even more shoddy and disreputable than the lobby. But I hardly had time to look around. He grabbed my shoulders, threw me on the bed and dived on top of me. If I had pause for any thought at all—other than shock and fear—it was that someone so totally soused could still have such strength and energy. I kicked and squirmed and pummeled him. He was beyond reason. My protests were futile. My struggling was getting me nowhere. I didn't scream, for fear that my saviors— given the fact of this unsavory hotel—might be worse than my attacker. In full face of the terror that I might actually be raped, I uttered a plea from the primordial depths within me: "Please Brendan, don't! I'm a nice Jewish girl!"

Those words somehow hit him like a cold shower. He bolted upright. He sat primly on the edge of the bed and with one hand stroking my cheek, he said: "Well, for Jasus' sake! Why didn't ya say that in the first place?"

While I cringed and trembled in one corner of the room, Brendan paced the floor, suddenly sober and very intense. He expounded upon the uncanny parallels of the Irish and Jewish historical experience, of the years of persecution, of the Nazi subjugation of the Jews and the British subjugation of the Irish, of the oneness of our spirits and the similarities of our songs. As I began to relax we talked together about Bar Mitzvahs and wakes, about confession and Yom Kippur, about the Last Supper and the Passover Seder.

As dawn broke across the Manhattan skyline, Brendan walked me down to the street and put me in a taxicab. The next morning —or rather a few hours later—he arrived in my office as he promised. He sat on a few secretaries' laps, took a nap on my

couch and serenaded us all. But the next day he started writing
a book about his love affair with New York City, called *Brendan
Behan's New York*. From that day until the day he died, we
were dear and special friends. And never a word was said
about the inauspicious, almost cataclysmic way that our friendship had begun in a grimy hotel in the wee small hours of the
morning.

The sentence that turned this potentially horrendous sexual
experience into just a charming anecdote was "I'm a nice Jewish
girl." I'll wager a year's salary that there isn't another man alive
for whom that sentence would have such a potent sobering effect.
However, because it was true for me at that moment to utter it
in desperate anguish and because of Behan's special sensitivity,
that line worked. Whether virginity or selective sexuality is your
goal, you are bound to have need of the perfect sentence to
extricate yourself from sticky sexual encounters. But don't bother
memorizing some all-purpose put-off formula. You'll be wasting
valuable gray matter.

What's your stand on sex?

When business relationships cross that fine line and become
sexual relationships—or incipient sexual ones—the unexpected is
the rule. Those halcyon days on the campus when Saturday-
night dates, dormitory curfews and a watchful society of contemporaries kept romantic matters simple are a far cry from the
subtleties of business liaisons. Any secretary who has ever accompanied her boss on a business trip, any girl who has stayed
after hours to work out a problem with a colleague, any business-
woman who has to entertain clients after 6 P.M. can corroborate
my claim: the only known quantity in these situations is your
own mind—and sometimes not even that.

We all try to make rules for ourselves to live by and they are invariably as hard to stick to as any batch of New Year's resolutions. Still, in my opinion, one above all others is an absolute, immutable dictum for any woman who values herself as a productive human being and who cares about her professional future. Don't sex around in your bread-and-butter bailiwick. Call it prudish, reactionary or unhip. I'll still swear by that commandment. Define the perimeters of your professional circle and draw the line on sexual adventure right there. That takes in office staff with whom you have direct dealings, men whom you negotiate with, meet with, sell for, sell to, think up ideas for, get ideas from, talk money with, get paid by, sign contracts with, attend conferences, conventions or committee meetings with, do favors for or accept favors from. (Keep calm. There are still plenty of other men left, if you'll just stop to think about it.)

To be sure, there is that one-in-a-thousand girl who makes it with her boss and survives on the job after the romance goes splitsville. Maybe one in ten thousand ends up with a bigger job as a result of the affair. And perhaps one in fifty thousand lands the boss as a husband to boot. But unless you are an incorrigible gambler and have an unfailing lucky streak, I would strongly suggest that you cool it. The worst tales of woe have been told to me by businesswomen who tried to buck the statistics. All the seeming advantages of a cozy corporate affair aren't worth the on-the-job wound licking when the romance goes bust.

One woman's story

An exemplary story was told to me by a girl I'll call Cheryl. She held an enviable, high-paying job in a large city as the assistant to the mayor's press secretary. She helped set up press conferences, worked on early drafts of the mayor's speeches and was assigned to do research on a variety of local issues from street signs to slum clearance. Cheryl's experience was special in that both she and her boss had just emerged from the divorce courts in their separate marriages when Cheryl started on the job. The press secretary, whom I'll call Michael, was a moody, intense man, some twelve years older than Cheryl. She was twenty-four at the time and thoroughly devoted to her career. Here's how she describes the beginning:

"I was ripe for an affair with Michael from the day I started to work for him. My divorce had left me eager to prove myself capable of a successful relationship with a man and hungry for someone to make me feel desirable. In the daily work situation I saw Michael in his very best light. He seemed so strong. He was confident. He seemed to me to be brilliant at his work— handling people in the mayor's office so deftly, always unruffled by any amount of confusion. I admired his creativity, his maturity, his quiet good manners. I suppose I was in love with him for six months before he noticed I was alive."

This last statement was rather hard to believe since Cheryl is a highly noticeable, well-built blonde. She went on to describe their working relationship.

"We really had to keep strictly to business because there was always such a bustle of events—always questions from the press to field and a mountain of reports to prepare. I was at Michael's beck and call, though our offices were fairly far apart on different floors at the City Hall.

"After six months or so I found myself reacting with all the standard symptoms whenever he came into my office. I blushed, trembled and hoped desperately to please him in my work and in my appearance. Finally, I admitted to myself that if he didn't make a move—in fact, if he didn't kiss me soon, I'd have to quit the job or else I'd go crazy."

I interrupted Cheryl's story to say that this sounded pretty melodramatic. At which point, another girl who was listening to our conversation chimed in: "It's not at all melodramatic. Haven't you ever had a private, unrequited love!"

Faced with such supportive emotionalism, I decided to shut up. Cheryl continued.

"At last, thank heavens, Michael asked me out to dinner. He didn't wait to kiss me when he took me home that night. He kissed me when he picked me up. It was the most startling, breathtaking kiss I'd ever had and I remember it even now.

"After that kiss we never went out to dinner at all. We had wine and cheese and salami at my house and we talked endlessly about our love. Because, you see, he *had* noticed me. He had been wanting me all the time. That night we built the foundations for our affair. I think they are important to mention because the nature of our business relationship contributed so much to the atmosphere and details of the entire romance.

"Michael decided that we would keep it all a secret. We would continue using Mr. and Miss in the office. We would go to work separately even though he would live with me. We would not ever confide our love to anyone we worked with. It would be ours alone and it would never interfere with our jobs.

"For eight months it was idyllic. I think we both loved the intrigue. When we took the same two weeks' vacation it was perfectly logical. Sort of like closing down the press relations department entirely. Michael and I both love skiing so we quickly agreed that Vermont would be perfect that February. I can't put into words what went wrong—but it was a *horrible* two weeks. I remember that on the plane to Vermont we were talking about marriage. On the plane going home we weren't even talking. Michael tried to reason with me but I couldn't even sort things out in my own mind. I just felt sad that our nice little love affair couldn't withstand two weeks away from the office. We both understood that it was finished.

"When we returned, Michael moved out of my apartment. Things were icy on the job between us, but I thought time would smooth the situation. Then Michael asked me to go out with him once more and I did. I hadn't lost all my feeling for him. I hadn't even understood what had happened between us. And it wasn't as though I were ditching him. He too was confused and uncertain about his feeling for me. That last rendezvous was a mistake from the start, I guess, because neither of us was really prepared to go to bat for the relationship. The reasoning attempts turned to bickering and the bickering to snarling until our silence became absolutely oppressive. He took me home.

"The next morning he called my office on the intercom and told me that if I didn't quit by three o'clock that afternoon he would fire me.

"You can just imagine how I reacted. I cried and pleaded with him. I loved my job and I told him I would work just as hard for him as I ever had. But he was adamant. He couldn't endure another day with me on the job. I had to leave. When I realized that it was hopeless I begged him for a recommendation so that I might get another job in city government. He absolutely refused. I handed in my resignation before lunch.

"Now I'm working in the research department of a local television station. It's a decent job but it's far from what I want. I enjoyed working for the city and I acquired certain skills that made me more valuable in that type of work than in any other. Michael fixed me good. He knows that it would take a lot of fancy footwork to explain why I left my job with him. He knows that I know that any telephone query from one of the other city departments to Michael would result in quite an earful. So here I am—blacklisted from any job in the city that I really want, all because I let my respect and adoration for my boss turn into a love affair. Even the postdivorce pains don't justify it. There were enough men around to ease me back into a social life. Fixating on Michael as a strong, masculine savior was a big mistake for both of us."

When Cheryl finished her story there were not one but two eavesdroppers: the girl who had challenged me about unrequited love and another girl who had known Cheryl and had felt free to sit in on her story. Miss Unrequited Love was in complete agreement with Cheryl that the romance had been all wrong from the start. Miss U.L. had her own experience to back up Cheryl's. She had been a political campaign reporter for a local TV station. During the course of her travels around the country with a man on the news squad she had succumbed to the call of the libido. She described the sense of dislocation, of being in strange hotel rooms, of having lots of drinks before little bits of meals. The excitement of sharing in a political campaign translated itself easily into the kind of closeness one feels in a summer camp or at a private school. All the participants felt that we're-all-in-it-together camaraderie that strips away conventional constraints and hastens familiarity. The atmosphere was right for romantic entanglements that would seem out of the question back on the nine-to-five job.

Miss U.L. and her man had three weeks of unwedded bliss. Then the campaign was over and the bubble burst. Miss U.L. did not fit into the gentleman's plans back home at the studio— so out she went. No wonder she nodded emphatically at everything Cheryl had to say.

The third girl listening to this interview was nearly scandalized by the "commercial" view that the other two were taking. Number Three felt that the other two were ignoring the human relationship they had enjoyed while it lasted, and that all they retained was a mercenary bitterness about losing their jobs. In other words, Number Three was upset that the girls weren't more tragically brokenhearted instead of being brokenhearted but acutely aware, too, of being jobless.

You'll have to decide where you stand on the issue. I know for certain that I've come a long way from viewing us girls as love objects alone. I don't believe we should be man-oriented first and foremost *all* the time. If a romantic liaison looks poisonous for your career, it may well be described as harmful to your spirit as well. What's wrong with a little healthy regard for the future of your spirit? Why shouldn't we women be *intelligent* about love before we allow ourselves to become naturally emotional about love?

Keeping the office off limits

In many ways we do this already. We censor our impulses by deciding intellectually that we don't want to get mixed up with a married man or a man of another religion (if that matters to us), a doctor (if we don't want to share a man with middle-of-the-night measles cases), or a truck driver (if we're snobby). Why it is any less "female" to intellectualize in one more area? Why *not* nip in the bud an on-the-job romance which is likely to imperil the job when the sweet talk turns sour? I'm in favor of selective mating. And I defy anyone to prove that it's hardhearted or unfeminine to protect your feelings and to protect your job by staying clear of these *liaisons dangereuses*.

If it's not loss of the job entirely it's another one of many hazards that lie in wait for the girl who mixes business with pleasure too closely. One unfortunate girl had a sexual hang-up that should have remained her private problem. She was a fairly extreme masochist. I gather that she required a variety of "punishments" before she could respond sexually. She asked her beau to slap her, tie her hands and legs, yank her hair and otherwise abuse her in order to prepare for the sex act.

Obviously, these are facts that I should not know about. However, because this girl dated a fellow in our office, not only I but twenty other people heard a full report. The young man was so completely shocked and repelled by the girl that he seemed to consider her an abomination which he had to destroy. He was compulsive about describing her weird sexual practices. This was his catharsis. He seemed to cleanse himself of the experience by exposing the girl to shame and ridicule. No matter how understanding or open-minded any of us were, it was impossible to look at the girl without visualizing orgies she had known and without searching for bruises, welts and missing hanks of hair.

I'm not suggesting that you might have some sick sexual proclivities to hide. But there is a point to be made by this extreme case. Any romantic relationship is going to be more intimate and more revealing than an office relationship can possibly be. Even without sex in the picture, the dating game brings out the innards in all of us. A social date should be relaxed and warm and without tension. As soon as you introduce the third element—you, he *and* the business—you are cheating yourself of your freedom. Either you will be dependent upon the job relationship which binds you for conversation and compatibility, or you will count for excitement on the intrigue of the illicit union, as Cheryl did. Or the added element will inhibit your freedom to be yourself for fear of revealing too much of yourself as a woman to be able to operate effectively in the light of day as a businesswoman.

To retain that freedom requires only a small exercise in self-discipline. Unless you are terribly hard-up this year, you should look to parties, friends of friends, blind dates, clubs, adult edu-

cation, sailing lessons or even dating computers before you
launch a love relationship in or around the office.

I can hear you protesting: Do I have to let all those attractive men pass me by because of this lousy career I've chosen
for myself? No, you don't. First of all, if it's really a *lousy*
career it may not be worth worrying about. In that case, you
can jolly well forget building a specialty or fulfilling your talents
and just job hop from office to office to find a man. We've already
decided that that kind of goal belongs to another kind of girl.

But even if you are our kind of dedicated achiever you don't
have to cancel business contacts out entirely. They can be social
friends and even lovers, as long as an intimate relationship
with them—and its aftermath—will not affect your formal business dealings. This you'll have to play by ear. I played it right
most of the time when I was single, but in one notable instance
I was way off key.

In the days when New York City had six daily newspapers
I was very busy working with their various editors placing
stories about Bernard Geis Associates books, setting up author
interviews or selling excerpt or serialization rights to portions
of our books. One of these editors was single, older and quite
distinguished looking. He was just the sort of devil-may-care
individual that I felt was O.K. territory for mixing business and
pleasure. He was paternal enough with me so that I was not
concerned that sex might be a problem. He was too old for me
to consider him husband material—nearly thirty years my senior.
He was sophisticated about life and casual about his women.
I didn't mind being one of many female acquaintances. In fact,
there was safety in numbers where this *bon vivant* was concerned.

We dated fairly infrequently for almost two years. It was
really a delightful setup. I was apparently a presentable young
thing suitable as a date for supper-club opening nights and

dinners on the town. He was a pleasant, bright companion for the theatre. We had some friends in common but mostly the hard-nosed newspaper world and the soft-spoken publishing business were miles apart. Which made each of us interesting to the other.

We had a standing joke about sex: he played the satyr and I the frigid maiden. This jocular role-playing suited me just fine. It made for some funny skirmishes in my apartment at the end of an evening but there was never a scene or a fuss made when I said no.

Throughout the two years, we had dozens of occasions to talk on the telephone or to exchange letters or contracts. I did a brisk business of placing stories in his paper and he did well with the books he ran in serialized or quotation form. Our rare dates were arranged at the casual convenience of both of us and with no sweat or hard feelings if they couldn't be arranged. Whether I had dated him the night before or not for three months didn't matter in the least if a valid news or feature story had to be discussed. We operated on two separate planes. And then I got married.

When I told him about my marriage I remember thinking that his congratulatory comments were rather hollow and terse. But it would never have occurred to me then to draw a conclusion from that. In no way could our situation be considered a "Dear John." Yet the first time after my marriage that I had occasion to call him to alert him to a publication-date press party, he was unmistakably distant. He never came to the party. Nor did he assign a reporter to cover it. The next time I called, his assistant took my call and asked if he could "help" me. For three or four subsequent calls I dealt with the assistant. The fifth time, my friend answered his own phone. I confronted him with the brush off.

"Hey, why have you been avoiding me? I didn't know that married women were off limits to newsmen."

"I haven't been avoiding you, Letty," he answered in an annoyed voice. "What can I do for you?"

"You can do one thing for me," I said, still seeking the old kidding-around tone I had been accustomed to. "Be nice to me, pat me on the head and tell me everything is okay."

"Come on, kid. I haven't got all day," he barked. "What have you got? A book, an author, a statement of policy? What is it?"

I saw that it was curtains for the friendship. "Just tell me which of your editors I go to with a feature story on college entrance requirements and I'll be on my way," I said.

He gave me the man's name and we said good-by. Ever since then I've developed a list of special-interest editors and reporters on his paper and I approach them directly. I've given up on my old pal. His message came through loud and clear: old girl friends who get married—even casual, fun girl friends— aren't worth the time of day. There wasn't much I could do about it and I certainly wasn't going to apologize for my marriage. So that's where it stands. You can't mix business with pleasure forever, even when it's going great.

Still, you can see that certain relationships *are* possible within your business ken. After sizing up the dynamics of your own situation you'll be able to decide which of the men you meet through your job are datable and which are not. It may not last forever, but if you've assessed your position carefully, the end of the romance will not signal the end of your business dealings with that man or his company. I no longer parry and play with my friend the newspaper editor. But I haven't been closed off at the paper altogether. Therefore, my decision to date this particular business contact was not an improper one. I had seen him as a casual, lighthearted romantic interest and one with whom personal relations would not become cloying or serious. So when I became unfair game as a married woman, he could move on efficiently to his other girls and I could move on equally as efficiently to his other editors. Fair and square and no one got burned.

Married men make miserable risks

The burning is frequent and severe for girls who mess around with married men. I've warned you about that "Married Men Make the Best Lovers Syndrome" before. But it bears repeating. All the standard reasons apply: they rarely leave their wives to marry their lovers. They are usually guilty about their extracurricular activities. Married men can't be with you on Christmas Eve, on overnight hikes or in public places. Married men, generally speaking, are compulsive complainers about the wife who doesn't understand or who is lousy in bed or who spends all their money.

On top of these routine objections you must add a host of new ones if your married man is also a business associate of yours. He's going to be fearful of discovery, not only by his wife but by his higher-ups. In a conservative firm he may also dread the opprobrium of his colleagues. If you're a file clerk and he's a vice president he may be even more eager to hide the relationship. He may be psyched up about taking advantage of you at the same time as he suspects that you may be using him. If the tables are turned and you're the v.p. while he is a lowly copywriter, *you* are going to question *his* motives.

The positions each of you occupy will determine what the likelihood is that you may meet his wife. But if it is at all within the realm of possibility that you and she be thrown together at a party, consider just how mortified you might be.

I have never understood the attitude of some girls who blithely date married men all the time. I can't imagine how they can repress the existence of the wife. I can't believe that one woman can be so lacking in empathy for another as to be oblivious of the poor wife's point of view. Certainly, no single woman is responsible for the condition of a man's marriage. But to allow and encourage the husband in his office dalliances is, in my opinion, a conscious contribution to someone else's misery. I would never want to feel in the least bit responsible for a wife's anguish. I would not want to think of myself as the catalyst for a father's alienation from his kids. Let them wreck their marriage themselves. I wouldn't want to play the vaguest role in hastening the wreckage. Nor would I care to feel at fault if a guy's career falters, if he loses his stamina and stability from leading a double life or if he loses his job altogether.

Married men are a foremost occupational hazard in the upper reaches of a man's world. They tend to slip into flirtations almost as a natural extension of their power and confidence on the job. They sometimes feel justified in fooling around a little now that all the tough, slaving years have paid off. Some married men who hold cushy jobs get carried away with their power. It's a short step from ordering a secretary to work late to ordering her to please more personal whims as well.

The married executive always has his work as an excuse to come home late. He can explain an out-of-town trip as a business necessity. For many girls he is a tempting temporary fling because he is so safely ineligible. Girls who feel no rush about making final life decisions find married bosses or associates most attractive. The combination of his status, his glamour, the unreal world of an office or a convention, the appeal of the forbidden and the fact that a lot of the nicest fellows around *are* married—all this makes for a potent brew.

It's a poisonous brew too and one which I never felt the

need to sample. There were plenty of fights, arguments and accusations along the way. But to my knowledge none of my beaux were somebody else's husband. One can never be sure, men being consummate liars about this sort of thing when it suits them. An easy faker once came my way at a trade exhibit. Since it was midsummer and his tanned left hand bore a white ring mark where his wedding band belonged, his fib didn't hold up for long.

The real tough nut is not the man who denies being married (a gambit which keeps him too busy fabricating to be dangerous) but the man who openly acknowledges his marriage and propagandizes against it. If he isn't defaming his wife, he is claiming that she and he have "an arrangement" regarding their separate affairs. He'll tell you that you are the one woman who makes him see how meaningless his marriage is. He'll rave about your business acumen and about how you can grasp the problem he carries on his shoulders and about how he can respect your opinions on his work. He'll pooh-pooh your reminders of morality. He'll challenge your "immature" ideals. He'll show impatience with your naïveté. You'll be cajoled and persuaded. You'll be assured that no one need ever know. Or you'll be guaranteed that your mutual relationship on the job or in the field will be unaffected.

Be prepared for all this propaganda and more. When I started meeting men as equals in business I was ready for anything. A spinster lady executive had filled my head with gothic tales of fallen women who had gone the route with married men. I was really overprimed. But preparedness stood me in good stead when I attended my first American Booksellers Association convention. Held once a year in Washington, D.C., this is the showplace for all book publishers' forthcoming publications. Bookstore owners and buyers, publishers and publishing executives of all stripes, journalists, guest authors and honored visitors from all over the country and abroad gather to savor the coming attractions. No less important than the business meetings and the displaying of wares are the extracurricular activities of the convention: drinking, gossiping, drinking, carousing, drinking and carrying on in a manner that does not befit bookmen and *literati* at any other time of the year. It is more than a trade exhibit. It is a distinctly social event and the right to attend on behalf of one's company is a mark of executivehood in the book business. After several years, veterans of the convention admit to one another that it is basically a repetitious round of booth hopping and bar hopping. But the first convention one can legitimately attend is the highlight of a publishing person's life.

The unconventional confrontation

I went to my first convention two months after I had been promoted from assistant director to director of my department. I was just short of twenty-two years old. Believe it or not, I had never been on a trip alone. Though I had been away at college for four years, it was a far cry from a business trip to Washington, D.C.—by myself. Clearly this was my moment of truth. I was a responsible adult, on my own and expected to perform professional tasks in a professional way.

My mind was so intent upon the business of the convention that I was oblivious to the monkey-business aspects of three days in a strange city. Dutifully, I toured the various publishers' display booths, took copious notes on competitors' offerings, attended the working sessions and luncheon meetings, made friends with bookstore owners and talked to all and sundry about our company's biggest books for the coming season. When the exhibition hall closed for the day, the round of cocktail parties began. It was great fun to roam the halls of the hotel

with hordes of other publishing folk, clutching highballs like
wilted bouquets as we toured from suite to suite. If this was
business, long live the almighty buck. Who could possibly dislike
meeting old friends over a rolled anchovy canapé or making
new friends on the veranda of a hotel suite with the Washington Monument as a backdrop? A small group invited me to join
them for dinner, which I did gladly—not noticing until we were
getting into the taxicab that the six of us were paired off. I
ended up with a fairly good friend who was an editor in another
publishing house.

Throughout dinner Hank and I found lots to talk about. A
bottle of fine champagne on top of all those cocktails in the
hotel had made our little group quite jolly and garrulous. Hank
and I had a short but pleasant history of business dealings
together. We had negotiated a few contracts, shared a few
lunches in the past and gotten along famously. But nothing
prepared me for the burst of intimacy that he showered upon
me at the dinner table. I knew that he was married. I knew
him to be quite a respectable executive about whom there was
no red, hot or blue gossip. But the drinks, the champagne, the
freewheeling atmosphere and the three hundred miles from New
York combined to make Hank quite suddenly a dirty old man.

He whispered suggestively in my ear. He rested his hand on
my shoulder. He even pulled the old hand-on-the-thigh-under-
the-table bit. I may have been a babe in the woods but this
babe wasn't born yesterday. I saw trouble coming and by the
time it arrived I had thought it through to its logical conclusion.
I wasn't sure what kind of trouble it would be. But I knew
exactly what I was going to do.

All six of us left the restaurant and traveled back to the hotel
together. Then, as though we were all a bunch of high school
kids home from a dance, the other two couples went off for

their private good nights and Hank strongly led me toward
the elevator.

"I'll walk you to your room, baby," he said.

"Oh, that's all right, Hank," I ventured futilely. "Your room
is on the opposite side of the hotel. Go ahead. I'll make it
alone."

"Wouldn't dream of it, baby doll," he drawled. "These girl-
hungry guys would be all over you before you could get your
key out."

Getting my key out was the least of my worries. In fact,
I resolved to keep my key *in* my purse until Hank was safely
out of sight.

As we entered the elevator, Hank quipped to the elevator
operator, "Once around the park, driver. And keep your eyes
on the road."

The large charge he got out of that witticism lasted until we
reached the door to my room. I murmured, "Good night" and
extended my hand. He grabbed it and used the contact to pull
me against his chest. Of the gruesome details, you shall be
spared. Suffice it to say that it took ten minutes, forty-three
wrestling holds and every protestation I could think of before
Hank realized that I was having none of it. He had passed
through a fascinating variety of transformations before he gave
up. He was the rake-on-the-make; he was the smitten suitor; he
was the accusing and wounded gentleman who had been led on;
he was the bored, old married man desperate for companionship
and fun; he was the business colleague vaguely threatening a
schism between our companies if I didn't hand over the mer-
chandise—namely my body and soul.

Miraculously, through all of this, no other door in the corridor
opened and no publishing passers-by ambled down the hall.
So the entire confrontation was strictly between Hank and me.

Had it been witnessed, I'm not sure that this anecdote would have had the happy ending that it did.

After Hank exited, tail between the legs, so to speak, and the elevator doors closed, I extricated my key from my purse, opened the door, heaved a sigh of exhausted relief and went to bed. I couldn't begin to contemplate the "punishment" that an embittered, deflated Hank might decide to mete out to me the next day.

He found me at the breakfast table the next morning. I prepared for the first salvo of the vendetta.

"Thank God, one of us had her wits about her last night," he said, looking around to make sure that no one was close enough to hear. "I'm so ashamed of my behavior that I can only say thanks to you for not letting me make a complete fool of myself."

My utter disbelief kept me silent. Perhaps he thought I was still unconvinced. He continued his incredible apology:

"I'm only glad that my drunken alter ego was revealed only to you. At least you know me well enough to realize that it was the demon rum and not old Hank attempting to ravage you." He paused and smiled, searching me for a reaction.

Gladly, gratefully, I agreed with him. Of course I had realized that. That's why I didn't allow him to gratify that Mr. Hyde side of his nature. We both nodded confidently. We shook hands and walked together down to the exhibition hall to rejoin the convention activities. It was our secret.

Hank is still a friend. We've met countless times since that 1961 convention and we've never made reference to the jousting session. On two occasions Hank has been with his wife at publishing functions. He hasn't had a moment's qualm about introducing me to her and I have been able to look her square in the eye without the slightest guilt.

If Hank had been single, it might have been different. If I didn't consider a married man another woman's property, it might have been different. If I had been green enough to be intimidated by his threats of disaster for our business relationship or if I had been embarrassed enough to give in rather than cause a scene. . . .

But all those ifs are academic. I knew what I had to do. And I think I was right. It was more important to me to remain a lady by my own definition than to prove myself a woman by his.

To paraphrase the well-known line from *Naked City*, there are thousands of married-men stories in the business world. This is one of them. But the variations on the theme are endless.

A girl I know attended a huge open-house party at Fire Island one summer. Late into the night people clustered on the beach roasting marshmallows and drinking red wine. My friend sat in a circle, which included several other executives from her company and their wives and a few big-shot clients and their wives. My friend had a great affinity for a vice president of the company who sat beside her on the sand. They had an enthusiastic conversation about pop art and an even more impassioned discussion of the negative income tax, on which they both agreed. Others took part in the conversation, including the v.p.'s wife. But my friend knew that for that evening, for that moment, for that conversation, she and the man existed solely to hear the sound of each other's voice. The group broke up, left the beach and boarded the ferry to return to the mainland. While the vice president was buying ferry tickets, his wife came over to my friend. With great calm and intensity that spoke far louder than her words, the wife told my friend:

"You turned my husband on. I just wanted you to know that I know."

Whatever fantasies my friend may have had about herself and the company executive were dissipated when she heard that very gutsy sentence. By Monday morning she had forced herself to forget that moment on the beach.

Another girl I know encountered a very different sort of wife. When Cynthia met her boss's wife at a company boat ride, Mrs. Boss pulled her aside.

"I know that you are having an affair with my husband [Cynthia wasn't], and I know that my husband won't give you up [according to Cynthia, the man was as disinterested as he could be]."

Cynthia's eyes widened as the woman continued.

"If you won't give him up here and now, you'll just have to move in with us. I won't let him go—ever."

Cynthia denied that there was anything at all between her boss and herself. But the woman had convinced herself that an intrigue existed. Or perhaps she wanted to believe that there was a love affair so that she could be justified in proposing the *ménage a trois*.

Cynthia left the woman abruptly with no attempt at a courteous departure. She stayed on the opposite side of the boat for the duration of the boat ride. The next day she gave her boss two weeks' notice. The poor man is probably mystified to this day. He was a perfectly pleasant man to work for and Cynthia was advancing nicely in the company. But she had a bad case of wife fright. This was one married man she wouldn't tangle with. Even if he didn't know it, Cynthia would always feel that a dangerous triangle threatened to engulf her.

What about sex and the married woman executive? Either I'm not too well versed on the subject or there just aren't that many wives who play around. (Three cheers for working wives!) The only dirt that's ever been dished around within my hearing is pretty tame dirt, really. There's one woman who admits that her husband is kept actively interested in her sexually by simply knowing that other men whom she meets in business are leching after his own wife. She plays to his need. She feels that it's natural for her husband to want what other men long for. So she regularly brings home stories of advances made toward her or of propositions she has had—whether she has had them or not.

Another woman blurted out to me that if she had to depend on her husband's attentions—not sexual but emotional attentions —she would be a frustrated, introverted mess. This girl thrives on men's compliments. She encourages flirtations and she basks in situations where she plays the desirable woman fending off unrequited lovers. So far, she claims she's a faithful wife. It's just a game with her and she's positive that it's a sensible accommodation to a husband who is the aloof undemonstrative type.

You set the tone and send the message

Each of us evolves a method of keeping sex on a level where it can be dealt with realistically. Each of us decides which are compromising situations and which aren't. We sharpen our antenna to either warm up the men on the make or to cool them down, depending on our own proclivities. Single women have to decide who to date in the business world, who to sleep with and who to steer clear of. Married women, if they are anything like me, protect the dignity of their marriage above all else. It's not hard to get your message across. And it doesn't have to be hurtful either. Here's a perfect guiding example for married lady executives. It happened to me just after the birth of my third child.

The man was very important to my company. The hour was very, very late, after a business meeting that had stretched into the night. It was delightful to relax with a drink after hours of business hassling, some of it high pressure. It was unwinding to have music, a dance floor and a chance to work off the stiffness

I felt from sitting in one seat for five hours. Everyone else had gone home. I was in a strange city and the meeting had taken place in a board room in my own hotel. It was quite natural for this man to invite me to have a nightcap in the hotel's supper club.

After our drinks were served I made some relaxed comment about the issues resolved at the conference. The man was sitting very close to me. He said he didn't want to talk business. I felt him staring at me.

"You look lovely tonight," he said.

"Thanks," I said.

"Short skirts look especially well on a girl with legs like yours," he said.

Uh-oh, I said to myself. Here comes trouble. But it wasn't panic time. I knew that whatever I did with the rest of the evening, I could not risk insulting him. As I said, he was *very* important to the company. But I was damned if I was going to be pyschologically blackmailed. I was innocent and direct. If he was going to be personal enough to comment on my legs, he was going to get a dose of my idea of getting personal.

"It's absolutely amazing how a girl's figure comes back so soon after childbirth," I answered. "Not only my legs, but all over. You should have seen my silhouette ten weeks ago. I was a carbon copy of the Little King."

He smiled wanly.

"You have children, don't you?" I continued.

"Yes, I do. They're away at camp," he volunteered for no apparent reason.

Whether he liked it or not, I had placed into the record several essential facts, like our marriages and our children. It's a bit awkward to press a seduction when labor pains and children's camps are the topic of conversation.

But the man had perseverance, you had to say that for him. In the midst of my quiz about his kids, he cut me short: "Let's dance," he said, taking my hand and leading me onto the dance floor.

For the first few numbers we were separated as a result of the up-tempo rock numbers that the band was playing. My escort did a fair approximation of the bugaloo, while all the time sizing me up like a race horse on the auction block.

Then the beat changed and, alas, it was time for a medley of good old-fashioned fox trots or whatever serious boy-girl dancing is nowadays called. The man held me very close, pressed his cheek against my hair and kind of nuzzled in. If I had any doubt that I might have been imagining his intentions, there was no further room for question. In fact, there was no room for deep breathing. He undulated, hummed in my ear and caressed my fingers. It was the kind of dancing that should be against the law for nonconsenting adults.

Did I push him away? Did I tell him to stop? Did I turn on my heel and walk off the dance floor? Did I say, "What the hell do you think you're doing" or "You have some nerve" or similar appalled statements? I did not. Any of these actions would have been out of place. There would have been no facing him tomorrow. And there would have to be a tomorrow.

"You're a splendid dancer," I said.

"Well, I enjoy it," he whispered, lips to my ear.

"Were you at that marvelous publication-day party that —— gave for —— last year?" I mentioned the name of a big publisher and a very famous author known for his hot pants.

"No, I missed that one," the man answered.

"Then you missed a once-in-a-lifetime scene. Mr. —— prowled that dance floor like a mongrel smelling out bitches in heat. All of us appeared to be engrossed in conversation while we were really unabashed voyeurs, keeping our eyes on Mr. —— as he worked his way around that dance floor."

"What was he doing?" my partner asked.

"He was making a spectacle of himself," I said brightly. "He pinched every behind within reach. He danced obscenely with any woman who couldn't escape him. Believe me, his gyrations made Elvis Presley look like a ballet dancer."

The man laughed. But at the same time I felt him relax his grip around my waist.

"I can't dance in a public place to this day without thinking of that party," I said smiling. "If Mr. —— ever had any stature, he lost it that night."

The man was facing me by this time. There was a decent distance between us. During the rest of the dance set we talked about that famous author and about other authors, books and publishers. I was home free. Without embarrassing him I believe I had established how I felt about lechery. I had ridiculed another man and through him my escort spared himself direct ridicule and eventual rejection.

We parted company in the lobby of the hotel. Our good-by was marked by a handshake and an exchange of smiles. Nobody was hurt. Two civilized people had parried and the better instincts of both had won. The sound of the human voice making sense is far more compelling than the call of the wild libido—any day of the week.

7.

Executive sweets

*N*ow that you're securely executivized we have to make sure that you can sit back and savor the fruits of your labors while still fulfilling your functions "manfully." Are you ready for all the fun, excitement and stimulation that a job can offer when a girl is prepared to relax and enjoy it?

It's my feeling that the sky does not have to be the limit. There *is* a moment when you can stop making it and start basking in your hard-won success and raking in the rewards. I, for one, have no desire to get any higher up the business ladder than I already am. Naturally, I hope to continue to grow in my job, to perform it more efficiently with each year, to be more imaginative and more creative with each new project. But I don't want to be president of a company or to be the first woman millionaire on my block. You could say that I've rechanneled my vertical aspirations into horizontal aspirations. This satisfied attitude about the status quo happens to be right for me. You may never feel like saying "uncle" to your career progress. By all means, press onward and upward. In my lexicon, status is not a nasty word. It's a thoroughly understandable human need—like food, clothing and shelter.

Raising the subject of a raise

Before shimmying into all those silky fringe benefits, let's be
sure that you're earning what you should be. You're the best
judge of that. You should know what is the going rate for a
comparable position. Measure yourself against people within
the company who hold jobs of equal responsibility as well as
against colleagues in your industry who work for competitive
companies.

It's not always easy to determine the pay scale no matter
how you may be intertwined with the grapevine. Perhaps the
best source of information is a trade organization. As secretary
of the Publishers' Publicity Association, I initiated a survey of
my fellow publicity directors to ferret out the facts on behalf
of all of us. Thanks to those unsigned questionnaires, our mem-
bership now knows the average salary for departmental directors as well as such useful tidbits as who is getting how much
in the way of profit sharing, stock options and bonuses.

You should check out whether or not men on your level are
generally better paid and what leverage you have to right the
inequities. You should try as far as possible to psyche out the
situation so that you don't ask for a raise the same week that
your boss has asked his boss for a raise or the same month that
the company suffered the loss of its biggest client.

Companies with well-established periodic wage reviews or
automatic increases are generally large, impersonal operations
that are less than sanguine about individual requests for raises.
But I've known women who have cracked even the toughest
of these fortresses—simply by threatening to leave if more money
wasn't forthcoming.

There's always the ghastly possibility that the answer will be a flat no. Let's assume that you've been turned down for reasons having nothing to do with your being a woman. The company can't afford it at this time. The position doesn't rate any more money. You haven't been with the company long enough.

This is your moment of truth. You, the foresighted female, will have considered this contingency before you went before the boss's bench. You will have decided in advance whether you are prepared to stay on without the increase. If you are, then you had better soften your approach so that your position is not untenable and your face can be saved.

You might appear as honestly disappointed as you feel when you hear that absolute no. But you should be ready with a calm transitional response. Something like, "Well, I understand the situation, Mr. Fulton, but I do hope that you'll keep my request in mind for the future." Exit without rancor and chart your next move in accordance with your prior resolve. Will you stick it out until Mr. Fulton comes through with a raise no matter when it materializes or how much it turns out to be? Or will you scribble a little note on your calendar for six months hence: "If no raise yet, look for new job." I'd do the latter. And more important, I would think through my total strategy *before* I stepped foot into Mr. Fulton's office.

Actually, I have never yet asked for a raise without first deciding in advance that I would either get it or get out. I haven't always gotten it on the spot. But at the very least I have gotten a guarantee that on a certain date in the not-too-distant future my paycheck would reflect a pleasant change of numerals.

Obviously, the willingness to leave, if it comes to that, is a girl's ace in the hole. You may not want it to come to that, however, and you may still feel that you *need* more money. Be ready to fight for it if his protestations are arguable. Whether you need a raise because you really need it or whether you need it to keep you feeling happy and satisfied is your business. Nobody in America who is not on the welfare roles is paid according to his financial needs. Remind your boss of that the minute he makes noises about your not being the head of a household. This is a free enterprise system right? We value performance, right? We pay salaries without regard for who has the sick mother at home, who has the million-dollar inheritance or who has the biggest mortgage payments, right?

Right. But only to a point. The single-woman executive and the working wife or mother executive who ask for a raise bring out the beastly double standard with banners flying. Don't let anyone put you down with pat answers. You need the money because you are worth it. Insist upon being judged on that basis alone.

Be prepared to prove your worth with ready examples. It's a crummy spot to be in but quite often a superior feels that the supplicating employee will back down when forced to catalogue her virtues. I am convinced that the time you ask for a raise is the time you throw humility to the winds. Sing your own praises to the skies. Single out isolated instances of your brilliance which may have slipped his mind. Inform him that you are painfully aware of how underpaid you are compared to the gal who had your job before you. If it's believable (and especially if it's true), let him know that you have had job offers from other companies. Make it crystal clear to him that you won't be happy if you're turned down and let him suspect that you wouldn't think twice about leaving if your very reasonable request is spurned.

In my case, I've gotten enough raises to keep me content for the time being. I'm sitting pretty at this level and I'm using my energy for on-the-job expansion and enjoyment instead of job-to-job movement. If you're at all like me, you'll recognize the perfect employment slot when you fall into it. And you may decide to be one of those fortunate working women who chalks up forty years on the same job and never once calls it a rut.

After all, what I've been talking about in this book is self-actualization. I haven't been lauding money and fancy titles for their own sake. Realizing your potential is what matters. Fulfilling your expectations matters. Using your talent or developing new abilities matters. Being interested in what you do each and every day matters most of all. And even if you don't do it for a living—even if you're being supported by a Mellon or a young Andrew Carnegie—you're doing a job to feel alive. Making a living doesn't cancel out living.

The combination of stimulating work and exciting fringe benefits makes Jane a happy and cheerful girl. A dull, monotonous job chained to the same desk makes Jane a dull dame. Anyone who doesn't like travel, parties, tasteful surroundings, good food and intelligent people should have her head examined. Nobody's saying these should be your deepest values. But they are nice decorative fringes on the tapestry of your life.

Have curiosity, will travel

They used to say "Join the Navy and see the world." I joined a book publishing company and I've seen seven European cities and eleven American ones on company money. I've traveled the way no tourist can. When you're in London on business you learn pounds, shillings and pence for more than the arithmetic of the porter's tip. You're involved, however modestly, with the economy of the nation. You care whether the government is Labour or Conservative. You understand what the devaluation of the pound really means in terms of United States trade because it hits *your* company in its British pocketbook. You dine in people's homes and you take tea in their offices. You hear the language spoken in its true context, not just over the taxicab divider. Someone will always take you to Trafalgar Square. On your own you can sneak away to watch the changing of the guards or tour the Tower of London. You have everything the tourist has and much, much more. You're seeing the town with a business friend who lives there and knows it as you know the "In" places back home. How many tourists are invited to costume parties in London? How many end up in a remote Chinese restaurant with French-speaking waiters? How many could join a student discussion group on the night that they debated the American involvement in Vietnam?

Because I was traveling for my company I spoke to Roberto Rossellini in Rome. Only on the telephone, though. He said he couldn't see me because he had a cold and his nose was rough and red from constantly blowing it. Honest. That was the reason he gave. Unsightly nose.

So I went to his lawyer's villa instead. And I doubt that Rossellini's digs could have topped the lawyer's home: marble floors, ancient pillars, terrazzo tiles from the time of the Caesars and a view of the seven hills of Rome.

In Paris, a publisher took me to a three-level club where we dined on each course amid a different décor, first Russian cuisine, then classical French, then to the basement, or *cave*, where an American jazz combo accompanied our dessert, coffee and Cointreau.

Another French businessman took me into the then turbulent Algerian section of the city where we went to the wildest, most elegant homosexual nightclub that could possibly exist on the face of the earth. No tourist could have found that place in a guidebook.

In Amsterdam, I had dinner with a publisher and his parents, who had survived the Nazi occupation of Holland. They told me the truth about those beautiful tulips of the Netherlands. The Dutch despise tulips. During the wartime occupation, when the Germans starved them and took their crops, the Dutch were reduced to eating tulip bulbs for survival. They have never forgotten.

In Spain, I became deathly ill with intestinal poisoning. Business friends found me a German doctor who spoke only German, Yiddish and Spanish, while I speak or understand only English, French or Hebrew. Somehow he treated me with the proper drugs and I survived. But the wife of my Barcelona agent slept on a cot in my hotel room, just in case.

A literary friend in Milan led me to a fabulous back-street shoe store where I bought magnificent Italian shoes for three dollars a pair.

Lest there be any misunderstanding, I must emphasize that I worked like crazy and wore my feet to a frazzle. It's fun to work in a foreign city. It's easy to accomplish all that your itinerary demands of you because everything is so new and different—and because you are conscious at every turn that through your business responsibilities you are learning something about the world.

A friend of mine doesn't have the sort of job that requires international travel but it does involve periodic trips in the States. Thanks to company business she gets to see her parents in Chicago at least twice a year at no cost to them or herself.

Another girl has to travel to Los Angeles every few months to check in with the main office of her theatrical agency. She stops off in Las Vegas for twenty-four hours every trip. With her uncanny knack for cleaning up at the crap tables this girl keeps herself in a four-hundred-dollar-a-month apartment with no roommates.

A lady executive with a lighting fixture company travels to Denmark every winter to survey the latest models available for import. She wings over to Paris for the spring couturier showings, picks up some real French brie and a dozen tins of snails and returns to New York fully equipped for The Good Life.

Get on the party line

So the job of your choosing doesn't necessitate travel more exotic than the bus ride from your house to the office. So what? You may be the type that gets airsick, anyway. Many jobs at the upper-management levels are absolute *open sesames* to the party scene. For the gregarious, social-minded girl this can be *the* ticket to fringe fun after hours and sometimes from nine to five as well.

In the best of all possible worlds you'll be holding down a position that allows you to think up a party, plan it and then go to it. Put on your party hat and use your head to make it a justifiable celebration in the company interest: a twenty-five-year anniversary, the launching of a new line, the passing of a new plateau in sales volume, the retirement of a third vice president or the coming of spring to your city—all of these have party potential if you package them right.

Use your departmental budget frugally and your imagination extravagantly to make marvelous, superspecial parties that everyone talks about for months afterward. Use your position as hostess to mix, meddle and meet anyone who captivates you.

I'll never forget the party given by the executive of a shipping company celebrating the opening of new freight routes or ports of call or some damn thing. The party was held on one of their company's freighters, of course. It was docked at a long wooden pier on the Hudson River, a postcard setting for a warm June night. We guests didn't just walk the gangplank to get aboard. After all, this was a freighter, not a passenger liner. We stepped into a thick rope net, six at a time. The net gathered around us and was drawn together at the top. Then a huge crane lifted the net high over the river and cranked us down into the hold of the ship like six bales of cotton or crates of bananas. Our entrance was a portent of things to come. The fidelity to the company theme made this party not only memorable but refreshing fun. All of us landlubbers sat on barrels and drank rum concoctions out of the ship's tin dinnerware. The loudspeaker made announcements typical of ship's calls. The waiters looked like merchant seamen and used language to match. The band played straight dance music on the bow of the ship and Latin rhythms at the stern. A helluva good time was had by all and there were a lot of drunken sailors in the net on the way out.

Our own party-giving experiences have been marked by a flamboyance and inventiveness that come more from the kind of books we publish than from anything we do to consciously make a zingy party. Remember the old saying: inside every fat man is a thin man yearning to come out. In the same way, inside every good product or project is a great party idea yearning to be set in motion.

When we published Harpo Marx's autobiography we picked up on Harpo's reminiscences about being a member of the Algonquin Roundtable, the famous ad hoc salon where *New Yorker* writers, pundits, critics and authors gathered to play games and discuss events of the day. So we chose the Algonquin Hotel as the scene of the party. In the book, Harpo described loving black jelly beans as a child and eating hard-boiled eggs in the kitchen of Mama Marx's home. So we served mountains of black jelly beans and platters of hard-boiled eggs instead of the hot and cold running hors d'oeuvres offered up at most publication-date parties. Harpo was there with his blond wig, his horn and his harp. Margaret Dumont, who regularly played the lady foil in Marx Brothers movies, came, looking as haughty and shocked as she always did in the films. Hedda Hopper was there in one of her absurd hats. Everyone was offered a Harpo wig and a pluck at the harp strings. The clock had rolled back to 1934 or thereabouts—and everyone loved it.

For the publication party celebrating Floyd Patterson's autobiography *Victory Over Myself*, we chartered a bus with a bar in the back to transport a crazy crew of sportswriters and book critics up to Floyd's training camp, about fifty miles from the city. The denizens of the sport pages and the book-review columns made strange busfellows and provided good copy for each other's feature stories. At the training camp in the woods of upstate New York our guests ate thick sandwiches catered by the famous sports and show-business hangout, the Stage Delicatessen. The book critics jabbed playfully at the punching bags, skipped rope gingerly and watched Patterson go a few rounds with his sparring partner. The sports reporters marveled at Floyd Patterson, the author. They listened to the sociological analyses offered up by the "intellectual" contingent to explain Patterson's sensitivity, his eloquence, his victory over his childhood environment. It was more than a party. It was a happening, before Happenings were invented.

When we published a fitness-and-exercise book by Bonnie Prudden, we invited the press, broadcasters and friends to a publication party in the form of a lecture-demonstration. Bonnie was on the stage in bright leotards and tights. Before ten minutes had elapsed she had all our business-suited guests doing pushups in their chairs and even trying a few of the "sexercises" from a provocative chapter in the book. The audience worked up a fierce thirst for the martinis that followed.

In the fall of 1969 we celebrated our company's tenth anniversary with an open housewarming. We took the "warming" part quite literally. Because our newly expanded, brightly decorated offices feature a real brass fireman's pole that we use to slide from the fifth floor to the fourth floor, we hit upon a firehouse theme. We sent out invitations with scorched edges and a drawing of flamboyant celebrants around a fire pole. We printed up shiny red matchbooks with the message "I had a hot time at BGA's Tenth Anniversary Party." Our tablecloths were red, and red carnations were everywhere—including a dozen or more tucked into the metal water sculpture in the reception room.

Red plastic fire hats were handed out as favors for guests to take home to the kids. Best of all, we had a New York City fireman stationed at the top of the fire pole to provide professional instruction to all those gutsy enough to take a trip down the pole.

Among those on hand to record these history-making descents was a television film crew. These cameramen couldn't believe their luck at having drawn such an assignment. We couldn't believe our luck at having attracted so many willing pole sliders. From an ex-cabinet member in the Eisenhower administration to Helen Gurley Brown, from a white-haired dignified fellow publisher to a kooky blonde in a see-through harem suit, they slithered, slid and squeaked down the fire pole to the delight of onlookers at the party and millions of television viewers who enjoyed the party via TV-news coverage later that night.

In our opinion, it was the fireman's ball to end them all!

Movie companies, art galleries and other subject-oriented businesses have hosted talk-of-the-town parties that were suggested by the movie or the works of art. Who can top the gallery that was exhibiting *meat art,* i.e., raw meat which had been designated an art form by the artist? They threw a steak dinner party. But, natch!

To launch the movie *Hot Millions,* the studio's publicists

took over the Chase Manhattan Bank after banking hours. It was the first time in recorded history that liquor was served through the tellers' cages and drink orders were taken on withdrawal slips.

If you can find no excuse or no logical extension of your duties that would allow party giving, there's always party going. Business people make a habit of giving parties for one another and they love to invite young lady executives.

Be a joiner

Parties aren't your speed? O.K., there are still other executive sweets to suit your craving. You're a professional now, so you're eligible to join associations, clubs, luncheon groups and seminars. These are good for all sorts of needs: your need to commiserate, your need to "borrow" ideas when your creative well runs dry, your need to see new faces with a ready-made subject available to make those faces speak to you and even, perhaps, your need to learn from others some basics of the profession that you missed on your fast climb.

For those who agree with my prohibitions about sex in the company or with close colleagues, the professional association might provide the safest, quickest route to meeting eligible men with similar interests. A cooking magazine editor may have to swear off literary agents, restaurateurs, food company execs, cookbook authors and coworkers. But she can have smooth sailing in a romance with a male editor from a sports magazine. Their paths cross only in the club. Whatever happens at the end of their affair cannot damage either of their performances on the job.

My T.K.O. of Hank notwithstanding, conventions *are* an exciting extra. If your executive position demands attendance at

some yearly sales conference, trade show, exhibit or convention
you should shout, "Have suitcase, will travel" and be up, up
and away. Men abound at these gatherings. If one of them
satisfies all your conditions of an okay date, then it's an added
bonus to do the town out of town. Meetings and conferences
rarely last into the night. It's a lucky girl who gets to tour
the sights of a new city with a willing escort.

Conventions afford a girl the opportunity to run through her
paces and to practice up for the all-by-herself traveling that
she may have to do in the future. Following the crowd is often
the fastest way to learn how things are done. You'll pick up
pointers from the other conventioneers. Do they take all their
meals at the same hotel where they're staying? Do they sign
the bill at the end of their stay or do they pay by cash or
credit card? How do your pals tip the chambermaid? Is it
standard operating procedure to take the limousine or airport
bus and then charge up a taxi to the home office? How much
free time do they take away from the convention in good
conscience and without guilt pangs?

And don't underestimate the educational potential of a convention. If your competitors are willing to exhibit the best
they have to offer, you'd be a dope to ignore their revelations.
A three-dimensional display that hits the spot for a girdle
manufacturer this year could provide the springboard to a
brilliant idea when you have to exhibit sectional furniture next
year.

The executive expense account

Most genies reside in urns and offer three wishes—if you rub
them the right way. An executive expense account goes the
genie one better. The wishes aren't necessarily limited to three

—and you don't have to do any rubbing. With such a willing spirit on your side be sure that you don't cheat the hand that feeds you. It's perfectly all right to order a filet mignon instead of chef's salad. (Who's to say you're not on a high-protein diet by doctor's orders?) But are you going to let Mr. Jones pick up the lunch check and then submit a petty cash voucher claiming that *you* took him? Are you going to meet your best girl friend for a swank dinner and then note on your Diners' Club voucher that you were playing host to a prospective buyer? You'll have to make your own morality on this score. The Internal Revenue Service would probably be the first to admit that their definition of a deductible "business" lunch is not shared by many.

Play it straight if you possibly can. Lies are not only embarrassing to substantiate and nearly impossible to remember six months later when the company is up for IRS audit—they aren't worthy of you or your position.

Most people feel entitled to charge the company for any expenses that would normally be incurred. For example, let's assume you have to attend a meeting across town. You are expected to travel by cab—perhaps not so much to benefit your status as to save your high-priced womanpower hours. It is a rainy, cold, miserable day. You can't get a taxi. You're going to be late if you don't start moving. So you walk part of the way through the storm and ride the rest of the distance in a steaming subway or overcrowded bus. Do you log in fifteen or twenty cents, which was your actual cost of transportation? Or do you hit petty cash for a $2 cab ride, which you figure would have been the approximate meter total? Everyone to whom I posed this question quickly answered, "Charge for the taxi rate it would normally have cost." These people aren't unscrupulous cheats. They simply reasoned that their discomfort and inconvenience in the rain—on their appointed round of company business—more than justified the two-dollar pay back.

Somehow I feel I can't charge up a $6 cab fare to the airport if my husband drives me to American Airlines on his way to the TWA terminal for his own business trip on the same morning. On the other hand, I charge the company for the cost of my dinner and a cab home when I have to work very late at night.

A lady editor practices a Peter-pays-Paul procedure. She very often takes buses to business appointments, charges her expense account for the taxis she could have used and then applies the money to her Neediest Cases Fund. This allows her to take a really starving author to lunch twice a week while her expense allowance would only permit one such lavish meal. Lord knows how many writers she's kept alive and nourished singlehandedly!

I would buy a client or chief supplier a set of the Harvard Classics on the firm's charge—but I wouldn't get the boss a Christmas muffler with a portable battery via the company account.

These are sample guidelines. You're welcome to adapt them to your own code of ethics.

We've covered the big bonuses of executivehood—the physical and monetary comforts which accompany your rise to a position of some power in the business world. We haven't mentioned the less concrete, more subtle and more substantial rewards of that power. Like the freedom to exercise your imagination with a budget to back it up. Like the satisfaction of earning your wage by making a real contribution to your company's success. Like the pleasure of discovering bright people and giving them the kind of helping hand that others gave you. Like the feeling of expertise and skill and pride of performance that warms even the coldest days of winter.

Your job should give you interesting things to talk about in your personal life and the self-confidence to talk about your projects with animation and eloquence. It gives you a background against which you can evaluate a man's shop talk and maybe even surprise him with a solution to one of *his* business problems. It gives you an added reason to look smashing every day of the year. These are private joys and sensations that go to the heart of one's psychological well-being.

Still, that doesn't make the little extras any less important. Even an ideal marriage built solidly on love and trust can be immensely enhanced by shared jokes, fun vacations and economic security. Similarly, swinging fringe benefits are the icing on the employment cake. I'm frankly and inexorably in favor of bonuses *plus* profit sharing *plus* a salary that lets you play the market, invest in a discotheque, decorate in Ming dynasty antiques or buy *yourself* a Crown Russian sable. I think it's marvelous that a girl can charge up a twenty-dollar wash and set when she's on a business trip. I rejoice for the woman who gives a business cocktail party in her home and finds herself with nine opened bottles of Scotch left over. I can't find a thing wrong with the practice of exchanging business Christmas gifts when it nets me three gift certificates from Saks Fifth Avenue, a basket of avocados and the latest Beatles record.

I had a couch in my office before I had one in my home. The Barcelona cocktail table in my office costs more than we spent for all our dining-room furniture put together. My husband and I don't have a single magazine subscription at the house. I bring home twenty-three periodicals which come into my office every month on company subscriptions. Of course, I have to keep up with the print media as a responsibility of my job. But it still can't be classified as backbreaking work—and it can be classified as an executive extra.

I could go on and on—but you get the point. Why fight it. It's fun.

8.

See yourself as others see you

A Scandinavian actress not quite comfortable with the English language once said, "This film business is very rude and cruel. If you are a weak person it can destroy your mentals."

The same holds true for the business world in general. Whatever happens to a starlet on the way to stardom happens in microcosm to a girl who starts at the reception desk and has her sights set for the corner office. There's the pavement pounding—whether for a bit part in the right play or for a clerking job in the right company. There's the hard work, long hours, tough working conditions, constant competition; there's the bad luck and there's the big break; there are failures, self-doubts and wrong turns along the way. If you are a weak person it *can* destroy your mentals. And it can discourage you. All those men sitting pretty in a world they made for themselves. And all those women hurtling into the pie where there are only so many plums to be picked.

Protect your mentals, physicals and emotionals in the easiest way possible. Ask before you leap. Ask your French professor what he would want most in the department's secretary. Ask your father if he ever met a woman in business whom he liked and respected. Ask your ex-bosses (if you left them on amicable terms) for their experiences with women at top-management levels. Ask well-known businesswomen in your community how

they did it and particularly what were their pitfalls. A letter
to one of these limelight ladies might land you a personal
meeting (because she may be flattered *and* curious) and a lot
of advice. Ask employment agents to tip you off ahead of time
if they happen to be aware of the eccentricities and pet peeves
of the man who is going to interview you. (If he has a passion
for wine-red nail polish you might have time to pick up a
bottle and do your nails in the bus on the way to the interview
appointment.) Ask people who turn you down for jobs to be
honest with you about why you don't fit the bill. If they find
you faultless, that's super for your ego. If people are too considerate to tell you their true criticisms, you haven't lost anything. And if they do come up with a metatarsal arch for your
feet of clay, you'll have a better work posture as a result.

I've done a lot of asking in my time. Often I've been told
how others see me without my asking. It has all been for the
best, I think, even though there were moments when I had to
remind myself that criticism only hurts for a little while. When
it comes from someone who has your best interests at heart, the
hurt turns into gratitude.

A few chapters back I told you about the boss who couldn't
bring himself to send me as a company respresentative because
of my beatnik wardrobe. (Translation for the now generation:
a prehippie beatnik wore sandals, not bare feet, long hair but
no flowers woven into it, hand-wrought silver jewelry, not
Indian bells or fertility beads.) This boss may not have realized
it but he forced me to face a basic fact of life: I would have
to make minor compromises. I had to learn to live two lives
gracefully and with equal conviction. I didn't necessarily betray
my love of the "natural" (as I defined it) just by wearing heels
or light make-up to the office. Nobody was telling me to wear
a double strand of pearls to a jazz concert or an Italian knit
ensemble to an underground movie.

Be a follower first, a leader later

By seeing myself through my boss's eyes I was able to make the adjustment. It wasn't really too much to ask. He merely wanted me to dress for the role I had chosen to play. He was saying that my aspirations for my career and my fashion image just weren't compatible. So I brought the two together.

Now are you ready for the double reverse? On the subject of fashion or outward appearance there is an ironic twist of plot. As long as I was moving around from job to job, feeling my way and trying to please others as much as myself, I made a conscious effort to dress for the role. Once I felt my footing was firm and my position was solid, the picture changed. I found that I could indulge my somewhat unique tastes in fashion— and what's more, I found that the more individualistic my appearance became, the more everyone seemed to like it.

When I was riding my motor scooter to work I came into the office wearing culottes, heavy knee socks and a crash helmet. My boss thought the whole scene was marvelous. On hot summer days I can't stand shoes, so I walk around the office in bare feet. One day I rushed into the boss's office—shoeless. He happened to have a rabbi and a film producer with him at the time. I froze midway into the room, trying to bury my toes in the deep pile rug. Men, being men (even rabbis and *especially* film producers), the three of them did not content themselves with greeting my face. They noticed my naked feet instantly. I apologized, murmuring something about having broken the heel of my shoe in the escalator treads on the way up.

My boss said: "We don't have an escalator."

I said: "Well, I'm sorry for barging in barefooted in any case."

My boss said: "Don't be silly. I was just telling these gentle-
men that in this company we really kick off our shoes and get
down to business. You're the living proof of that."

The two visitors were very much amused, but in an affirmative
way. The whole atmosphere of the meeting became a bit
more relaxed from that touch of office irreverence.

A few years ago I stopped rolling my long hair up into a bun.
I stopped wearing clothes to fit the job and started wearing
clothes to fit my taste. It no longer seemed necessary to carry
on the pretense of being older than I really was. Miraculously,
nobody asked for my birth certificate upon seeing me in long,
straight hair. In fact, I was overjoyed that I'd evolved into
wearing what was the most natural look for me in time for
Rex Reed to interview me for a story in *Cosmopolitan* magazine.
He wrote: "She resembles the pink-cheeked, sunflower-haired
girls on old-fashioned Christmas cards, and talks with the exuberance of Dorothy on her way to Oz."

If I had still been playing the compromise role I had set out
for myself early in the game, his sprightly description—true or
not, it delighted me—might have read something like this: "She
resembles the rouged, chignoned girls on old-fashioned WAC
recruiting posters and talks with the exuberance of Jane Wyman
in *Johnny Belinda*."

So what's the answer? For me and for my estimate of the
business I am in, it was necessary to follow the advice of that
long-ago boss. For a while I *had* to adapt myself to what others
expected of me. Now I can wear four rings on one hand and a
leather mini-skirt. So can all the other girls in our company.
The time is right, the office is right and the boss approves.

Your total situation will determine how much of an adjustment you'll have to make in clothing, hair style and in general
demeanor. I don't think you would ever get away with a see-
through blouse at I.B.M. (But I'd love to know if I'm wrong.)

Until that day comes perhaps you'll discover, as I did, that adopting the standards of taste held by your superiors in the minor things in life—like your mode of dress—does not mean you're a sellout. It means you're adaptable and considerate *and* smart.

Basic office crimes: are you guilty?

Appearance is one small part of yourself as others see you. Certain behavioral patterns emerged in my talks with businessmen about the women in their world. Here, in direct quotes, are some of the complaints issued most frequently—and issued with expressions ranging from bug-eyed fury to bemused tolerance:

1. "Women don't turn off their electric typewriters, desk lamps and air conditioners at the end of the day. They act as though Daddy is still around to pay the electric bills."

2. "Why do so many girls leave paper coffee cups on their desks all day long? Cold coffee, floating cigarette butts and lipstick-stained cups lined up like soldiers on the secretaries' desks are aesthetically offensive."

3. "Girls take and make too many personal phone calls during the business day. And from what I overhear, the calls are not worth overhearing."

4. "I hate bowl-me-over perfumes concentrated in our small office."

5. "Women are too damned emotional. Why can't I criticize our female vice president to her face without getting that teary look and a choked voice? Our male vice presidents never cry."

6. "Women who are hell-bent on becoming executives are

too carnivorous and too devious. Women without executive ambitions are too passive and apathetic. Isn't there some middle ground?"

7. "A secretary is someone who should be a combination typist, stenographer, message-taker and file clerk. Why is it that all the girls for hire nowadays can't type, sten, message-take or find the Miscellaneous file under 'M.' Girls who think skills are declassé are only hurting themselves. They'll never get anywhere in the business world."

8. "I hate women who clutter their offices with shopping bags full of lunch-hour bargains. (And take two hours for 'lunch' to acquire those bargains.)"

9. "Girls are absolutely incapable of punctuality." (One lady advertising executive answers that with: "If a woman is late, all of a sudden this is a female trait; if a man is late, it's because he's so busy!")

10. "It's not fashionable to admit it but I'll always view a woman executive as someone whose job could have gone to a man. Women can work for gratification, for fun or for a lark. Men work for a living. It's nice for the gal who pulls down $20,000 a year in an executive position. But that's $20,000 that could have gone to a man with the serious responsibility of supporting a family. Girls had better understand this point of view. I'm not the only man who feels this way."

These ten complaints range from the perfidious to the profound. Some are inane; some are vitally important to you and to me. Working backwards, the number 10 statement is the most provocative.

A recent magazine article reports: "Statistics support the fact that male executives often do not feel comfortable about their female counterparts. In 1965, when the Harvard Business School surveyed one thousand businessmen, it found that forty-one percent of them viewed women executives with undisguised misgivings."

These misgivings were not explained. Partially, they may be due to the lingering male suspicion that women are never as capable as men. It may also be a well-founded fear of female emotionalism on the job. However, the sentiment expressed in the number 10 statement above is most likely at the root of the misgivings: resentment born of economic and professional competition. This kind of man believes that a man *needs* a job even if a woman *deserves* it.

No matter how you see yourself, you must realize that this kind of man is going to see you as the plunderer of sacred male territory. There is not much to be learned from a guy who has this primitive complaint about females in business. It doesn't leave you any room for self-improvement. Short of proving to him that you are a widow with six children and six years of back taxes to pay, he's going to be sure that you remain in that $85-a-week job because he's convinced you don't *need* anything more. And, of course, the "need" standard for job filling applies only to women. He'd never think of filling executive positions on the basis of need among the boys.

On the subject of number 9's beef about punctuality, I have only one thing to add to the ad lady's comment: if being on time matters, *anyone* can be on time. It may take psychoanalysis or self-discipline, but it can be done. Not all women are incapable of punctuality, despite the stereotype. I know two compulsively punctual girls who are far more annoying than the dawdlers. To my way of thinking, a guy concerned with punctuality to the minute and complete with time clock is a victim of poor toilet training. Show me an office with a time clock and I'll show you a cold, impersonal place to work. But I suppose more companies have punctuality rules than don't. If yours does, then you may as well take number 9's complaint

to heart. Set four alarm clocks in your bedroom or pay a friend
five dollars a month to call you every workday morning to be
sure you're awake. Don't be late more than once a month. It
gives all us girls a bad name.

Number 8 is right. Shopping bags look lousy propped against
your office wall or spilling their contents on the floor under
your desk. Put them in the cloak room, check room, closet or
whatever. And if there's no place to put them and you *have*
to buy that gilt-edged set of matched luggage during your
lunch hour, tell the store to send your purchases home direct.

For my rebuttal to number 7's harangue about secretarial
skills see chapter 2. I asked one of the men who shared this
complaint whether he had a secretary at the moment whose
skills were adequate. He said his secretary was terrific at everything—a real find. I asked him how long she had been with
him. He told me very proudly, "Eight years."

I asked him if he really thought that his gal's great skills had
"gotten her anywhere in the business world."

He blushed.

The middle ground that number 6 so wistfully pleads for is
the ground I hope we're tilling in this book. I share his hope
that there *is* an in-between girl who is aggressive and ambitious
but never ruthless—feminine and agreeable but never inert.

Before you let the lumps rise in your throat, before you let
your eyes brim full or your fury erupt, try very hard to see
yourself as a number-5-type man will see you. He may be
correct in his claim that male vice presidents never cry. But
who's to say that they wouldn't like to. The point is, however,
that they *don't*. I don't think this is because women have a
monopoly on tears. I've known men to cry at broken love affairs,
lost football games and movies about children or dogs. But I've
never yet seen a man choke up in a business contretemps. It's
not just that emotion is unmanly. Emotion of that sort in an

office is *unseemly*. It's just as much unlady-like as it is unmanly. It's unseemly for all of us.

Office politics upset a lot of women. The failure of a specific project or the denial of an executive privilege makes some girls pout for days. This is the kind of "emotionalism" that the men with complaint number 5 were objecting to.

I questioned the objecting males more fully: Did they mind squeals of excitement or enthusiasm about some company or personal triumph? No, they thought that brand of emotionalism was healthy and refreshing. A girl's ability to react viscerally to something happy is a quality to be admired. The men felt that very often they enjoyed the pleasure vicariously. The female reaction spoke for them.

Did they mind anger? No. Honest, fist-pounding anger about a lost client or a ruined piece of artwork was, again, understandable and easy to deal with. Anger in the face of some catty infighting was another matter. Men don't like to see it; they don't like to get involved.

Moods, crying, pouting, general ill-humor—these were the various counts under the indictment of emotionalism. We can't expect men in business to accept us for our brains and talents if we wear our hearts constantly on our sleeves. Certainly, if we are agonizing over a broken engagement we will be forgiven a few weeks of smudged make-up and several attacks of acute indigestion. But in a May-Day case such as a vanishing fiancé we owe it to our office colleagues to leave a hint around where all can see so that the typewriter repair man or the company sales manager doesn't feel he's the cause of our sudden outburst of hysterics. Wrap the fiancé's picture in black bunting and raise the engagement ring to half-mast in your pencil cup. But do send up a signal to get the innocent off the hook.

None of the complaining bosses interviewed asked us to be stoical masks in the face of personal tragedy. They only asked that we keep our more mercurial moods in check and that we save all but the most crucial emotional traumas for the folks at home. Your business relationships will involve criticism, conflict and defeat as well as victory. You have to deal with these relationships without tears. If you can't stand the heat, go back to the kitchen.

Number 4 is a frivolous complaint and I only include it here because it came up in a good many conversations with businessmen. We girls must have developed paralysis of the olfactory organs. I can't remember ever being aware of cheap or heavy perfume in an office. Still, I pass this peeve along to you as a reminder that moderation should be your guide in all behavior affecting the five senses of others with whom you work.

Number 3 hits me where I live. According to my standards, *everyone* makes too many personal phone calls on office time and money. I'm no goody-goody on the subject. I simply relate this practice to my own experience. If I returned home and found that my baby-sitter or my cleaning woman had spent an hour of her eight-hour day on my telephone I would hit the roof. Would you expect the guy who comes to clean your windows—and whom you are paying by the hour—to use your paid-for time for his calls to his bookie, girl friend or poker pals?

Lots of girls have justified this by reassuring me that the company is big and rich and certainly can afford a few extra dollars' worth of message units on the monthly bill. Ah yes, but if one girl justifies it so can the four hundred thirty-three other employees. If *all* of them call the dry cleaner, the grocer and Aunt Fannie—*voilá,* a hundred-thousand-dollar phone bill.

Number 2 is again a complaint with which any girl can sympathize. Maybe you can live with four cups of your *own* leftover coffee and a few bread crusts from lunch on a corner of your desk. But do you like to see the leavings of the girl in the next office?

I'll go out on a limb and say that there's an easy explanation for the fact that women are the worst offenders in the messy desk complaint. Could it be that we are used to food in its raw and unattractive state? Could it be that we just don't notice how nauseating a few strands of coleslaw and a pickle can look alongside an "In" box? As cooks we are perhaps *too* accustomed to seeing food in all states of disarray. Men are used to seeing the finished product on a gold-rimmed plate with a sprig of parsley. I know that I am now completely oblivious to the unadorned appearance of a raw chicken liver. My husband, on the other hand, was a great fan of chicken livers en brochette until he saw one naked and uncooked in a bowl on the counter.

Whether or not this explanation satisfies you, you'll just have to admit that the complaint is well-founded. It goes to the core of the messy-desk syndrome. If we strew leftover sandwiches and old coffee cups around our desks, we are probably also capable of spilling warm Coke on the annual report and letting cigarette ashes fall into the sample kit. We may learn to live with the wreckage but we're talking now of how others see us. If they see garbage on the surface, they're going to have good cause to wonder whether our sloppiness is indicative of deeper problems of disorganization. I know the head of a publishing company who is convinced that girls with messy desks are poor spellers, lacking in self-confidence and generally untrustworthy. I've warned a few of the women who work for him that a crumpled candy wrapper could be their undoing.

Beware, too, of the opposite extreme. In my office there is nothing more suspicious-looking than an antiseptic desk top. Girls who work with one paper on the desk at a time will have a job convincing us that they're producing. No man that I know objects to piles of correspondence stacked with reasonable neatness on the desk, a collection of articles to be read at some future time or file folders bulging from a desk rack. If somewhere on that desk there's a plant or a bud vase with a single carnation in it; if one cup of coffee is visible at a time; and if the owner of the desk can put her hands on a requested piece of paper in thirty seconds or less—then all is well.

The men who tendered complaint number 1 are really pleading for nothing more than consideration. On a corporate level, many of us claim that the impersonal atmosphere kills the human emotion of thoughtfulness. Turning off a typewriter, air conditioner or office light at the end of the business day is nothing more than a thoughtful act. Like not making personal phone calls, it shows some understanding of company overhead. If your office requires it of you—some skyscraper office buildings say hands off the lighting and air-conditioning equipment—then just train yourself to comply. Put up reminder cards on your bulletin board or tie a red string around your back space key. But try not to flounce out at five o'clock thinking that someone else will close up your shop for you.

In addition to the top ten offenses there are a myriad of DON'Ts mentioned perhaps less often but with equal fervor.

Don't reveal company troubles or gossip in public. Loyalty is something measured not in a raised right hand or a formal oath. It is a strict respect for company privacy and a zealous hatred of betrayal.

Don't complain when other departments don't follow through for you. Your superiors aren't interested in who sabotaged your stellar efforts. Go right to the problem and waste no time on the blame. If the shipping clerk is responsible for your missing a deadline, have a constructive talk with him. Tell him how important he is to the smooth functioning of your department. You'll be solving your problem directly, pleasantly and without hostile recriminations.

Don't open doors for yourself, light your own cigarette or put on your own coat if there's a man around willing and eager to do it. You may have acquired a "man-sized" job but you needn't take on a man's role. Little things *do* count—especially where the maintenance of femininity is concerned.

Don't cop out on the financial end of the business. Too many girls feel that accountancy or just basic familiarity with the economics of their own business is too complicated for them. Men object to this sort of resistance. A girl can't suddenly pull her femininity out of mothballs when she's not up to learning the facts and figures of the business. Do *you* know how much your company grossed last year? How about the overall budget of your department? Departmental overhead? Cost of manufacture for whatever item your company makes? Have you mastered *any* financial figures other than your own salary?

Don't use your underlings as sounding boards for personal problems. People who work for a woman boss have enough problems without shouldering the woman's personal disappointments or vendettas.

Don't flaunt your privileges around the office. It only makes it harder for your superior to do something for you the next time around. It hurts and embitters others and gives them an idea of what to demand for themselves.

And now a word from my staff . . .

Having thus counseled you against bragging, I am about to indulge my own swelled head for a moment. But in a very different context. A few months ago I sent the following memo to my secretary of seven years, Judy Schein, and to my recently hired assistant:

"For the book I'm writing I need an honest, complete report from you on what it's like to work for me.

"No kidding.

"Be specific and don't shy away from severe criticism. I can't guarantee that your comments will affect a change in me but they will be very helpful to my research. A few typed pages would be great. At your leisure."

My assistant provided her comments in bits and pieces over the course of months. She felt she was in no position to offer a full-scale boss portrait until we had worked together for a longer time. By the time she had been with me for a year, however, the comments mounted up. And though I've kept very loose track of them, it's clear that there are an equal number of pats and pans. The pats are nice but the pans are something we can all learn from.

She says I'm quick to criticize and quick to praise. But my criticisms are much harsher than my praise is gratifying. In other words, I suppose the bad aftertaste lasts longer than the pleasant one. And criticism is a demoralizing setback for someone who really means well.

According to her, I expect her to operate on the same supercharged batteries as I do. For someone like this girl whose metabolism or physical energies have a lower threshold of exhaustion I have come to realize that I tend to be too demanding. If I'm not tired I assume everyone else is still raring to go. This lack of sympathy is a fault I still find hard to correct. My assistant has to keep reminding me that after particularly hectic weeks of working at my pace she has had to catch up by sleeping through entire weekends with only a pause for a nodding meal or two.

She has also called me to task for my flaring temper, my tightfisted passion for expense-account economy and my breathing down her neck over deadline work. So, obviously, despite all my experience working for imperfect bosses I haven't mastered the art of being a perfect lady boss myself.

My secretary, Judy, has had her objectivity mellowed by years of close association. Here is Judy's reply verbatim. I'm shamelessly bragging about her memo because until I read it I truly had no idea of what kind of boss I've been to Judy over all these years. I think you'll understand why reading this was one of the most touching and gratifying things that has happened to me in my business life. (It also gave me the guts to write this chapter with some degree of confidence!)

Judy answered: "You've set a task before me that seems insurmountable. I've probably spent more time with you in the past seven years than with any other individual (including my husband, if we were to count the hours). At this point I have practically no idea of what you really look like or what you sound like—nor do I have trouble pronouncing your name. Therefore, questioning my thoughts on what it's like to work for you is sort of like questioning my thoughts on bus rides or bedmaking—so much a part of life that one never stops to think about it.

"Nevertheless, in the name of research, here goes:

"We've got to work under the basic assumption that if I found you a whip-carrying, slave-driving, ego-maniacal type boss, I certainly wouldn't have grown from puberty to adulthood under your direction. (Well, practically puberty.)

"Probably the biggest advantage of working for you (or for someone like you) is the knowledge that purpose is behind your every move. To see dreams become realities (in our case, creating best sellers) adds an excitement to *every* day. It's a lovely, secure, warm feeling to know that one's efforts are about to cause results and not just another way of getting through a day.

"You're a demanding boss, but I doubt that anyone would

object to working their tails to the bone when the person giving the orders is working even harder.

"You've a firm grasp of what you can expect from those working for you. Which benefits both of us because (a) you don't *usually* ask the impossible and (b) those working for you know that if something is asked of them, it can, in all probability, be done. (Imagine being asked the impossible, finding it just that, and then being told that you didn't try hard enough. Makes for low morale, to say the least.)

"Looking at it from another point of view, if you didn't know what to expect from me, I could probably take long lunches, read magazines and write letters between 9:30 and 5:30. (Of course, I'd probably be pounding the pavements before too long due to an acute case of boredom.)

"I think you're as fair as anyone can be. Certainly, you're always quick to praise. And almost as quick to berate. A nice combination and one that lets one know where one stands at all times!"

After I fell all over Judy in gratitude and affection I sent her back to her typewriter. "I must be doing *something* wrong," I told her. She returned the next day with this memo:

"So you want me to get really personal (and less flattering). Here are some of your quirks that I neglected to include in my original memo:

"(1) If I happen to sit back in my chair and relax for a minute (which I sometimes do, I admit), you have a tendency to panic. The reason as I see it is, if I have nothing to do then you haven't given me enough to do, therefore you're not doing enough. Since this reasoning sometimes comes in the midst of a holocaust of work—which is why I leaned back to relax for a minute in the first place—I see red.

"(2) Somehow you've never been able to master the intercom. Which, naturally, leads you to the only other means of inter-

office communication: yelling out your office door. The only
time this unique habit concerns me is when, returning from the
ladies' room, I realize that I'm hearing the end of what must
have been a ten-minute, fully detailed explanation of a new
project that you've been yelling out to me in my absence.
Makes me wonder how many times a day I don't catch the
ending—and therefore never know there was a beginning, either.

"(3) You always expect your coffee the *first* time you ask
for it.

"(4) You drink tea with cream."

All you alert readers out there probably picked one sentence
out of Judy's report and you're dying to confront me with it.
If I'm so big on job progress, why has Judy been with me for
seven years? That's as long as some antiquated indenture deeds
lasted. Why don't I practice my own precepts and give my loyal
secretary her freedom and a boost up the ladder?

The answer is: I have. *She* has refused to move onward and
upward. First I promoted her to be my assistant. But that wasn't
her bag. She didn't like making approaches to radio, television
and press people to book our authors for interviews. She just
isn't the pitchman type. She didn't like being tucked away in a
private office. She felt too remote from the action. She didn't
like being relieved of her typing responsibilities and various
other administrative chores. She felt too out of touch with day-
to-day activities.

So then I made her director of foreign rights. It simply
meant splintering off one of the four departments under my
aegis and giving Judy sole responsibility for it. But she didn't
want that either. Too limited. Too isolated from the publicity
fireworks in the rest of the department. She wasn't content
negotiating deals for Portuguese translation rights or checking in
with literary agents around the world.

Next I fired her for her own good. A leave of absence is a

better way of putting it, I suppose. But I really had in mind cutting the umbilical cord so that she might find herself in some other job or in some other field. Six months later she was back. In all honesty I thanked my patron saint for her return. But going a step further, I felt I had discharged my responsibility toward Judy's career. From that time on, I've left well enough alone. My own attempts to "liberate" Judy have cleared away my guilt at being given the gift of a totally loyal and devoted secretary. Judy has what she's most happy with and I have Judy right outside my door.

There's a great lesson in this personal anecdote. People like Judy are able to see themselves as others see them and *still* —in the final analysis—prefer to see themselves as they see themselves. Do you follow me?

Judy recognized that I saw tremendous potential in her. She knew that every opportunity was available to her to advance within the organization. She was always aware of the affection felt toward her by the other executives and she knew her promotions would have been celebrated by all. We see her as capable, beautiful, charming, efficient, smart and responsible. Perfect executive material. It all made sense—to everyone but Judy. She wanted to learn more, understand more, get more money, take on new activities, but stay put.

Her business cards which read "Director of Foreign Rights" sit in her top drawer. Her own correspondence bears whatever title seems applicable to the subject in the letter. She's completely oblivious to status symbols. She only wants the job to grow. She doesn't want to grow out of it. She values her personal life with her husband and she requires no major ego satisfactions in the office. She is content.

We in the company no longer try to impose our image of Judy upon her. She is flattered and pleased by everyone's confidence and encouragement. But she's one girl for whom "See yourself as others see you" is a futile inapplicable exercise.

I don't cite Judy's situation as a consolation prize for those readers who have come this far and still feel unmotivated to push for the executive heights. I mention it to show that there are many ways to make it in a man's world and all of the ways ultimately should come down to one's own choice of life style. Those of us who are eager to be decision makers should have the chance to prove ourselves able to perform those functions. Anyone who thrives on responsibility and blossoms under pressure should be given the opportunity to fulfill these needs. The upper reaches of man's fortress should open for these women.

But by the same token, girls who put a ceiling on their progress volitionally are not necessarily a living advertisement for the forces who want to keep women in their place. The system opened for Judy and she made the choice to stop at a point in time and space that suited her. Nobody put the screws to her ambition. She has gone as far as she wants to go. And to my way of thinking—in human subtleties and not in black-and-white terms—girls like Judy have "made it" just as legitimately as the first lady stockbroker to ever gain a seat on the stock exchange. Each in her own way has found satisfaction, gratification and the right to control her own professional destiny.

9.

*If you can't
stand the heat,
get back to the
kitchen*

*L*ast New Year's Eve my husband and I went to a party in the suburbs at which were many of his old college friends and their wives. In almost each case the couples had married immediately after graduation and the wives—all college educated—had become full-time housewives and mothers. My presence at this party seemed to challenge these nice ladies. It was as though my split-level life was an affront to their single-tracked home-mindedness. At first I suspected myself of my own female paranoia. But my husband corroborated the original impression. They *resented* me because I work as well as raise children and run a household. They were hostile, self-righteous and rather defensive. It would have been convenient if I had two children on the psychiatrist's couch. Then they could have pointed to cause and effect.

It's easy to dismiss a maverick with a yes, but. "Sure, she has an exciting job and an interesting social life. Yes, but look at those poor neglected children."

Unfortunately for their egos they know my children to be happy, well-behaved, bright and spirited kids. So where's their out? Well, in this particular gathering, the forces coalesced into a phalanx with the battle cry of "I love my children and home more than you do."

My final sense of relief and triumph came not from any brilliant putdown that I thought up. It came when one of the women let slip her true feelings. The dialogue is worth reporting only because it is so classic:

Wife A: How's your job, Letty?

Me: Marvelous. It's been an exciting season in publishing.

Wife A: It must be awful to leave your children for an office job.

Me: No, actually, I don't mind it. I work because I want to, not because I have to. The children are quite accustomed to my working.

Wife A: But, I mean, you have to leave them with a virtual *stranger*. Someone who couldn't possibly love them as much as a mother does.

Wife B: And what if some accident happened while you were working. I'd never forgive myself.

Me: Our baby-sitter is by no means a stranger. She's been with us since the twins were three months old. She lavishes love on them like crazy. I wouldn't leave my children with a woman unless I were absolutely positive that she would care for them just as well as I do. And as far as that illusive extra quality called mother love is concerned, the girls get that from me almost full-time when I *am* home.

Wife B: And what about accidents?

Me: Naturally, I can't say they won't happen. But thus far the only accidents we've had are those that have occurred while *I* was home. You can never be sure your child won't be run over when he's out for a walk with his grandmother but you don't forbid her to take him out for walks, do you?

Wife C: What I wouldn't like about working would be the loss of precious hours with my own children. No one can possibly contribute to my child's growth and experience the way I do. I want to be home every minute to watch my little girl develop and to teach her things and share in her discoveries. A baby-sitter can't do that!

Me: Tell me this: Do you ever go out shopping? Do you get your hair done? Do you clean your house, cook the meals, do the mending, visit with neighbors, read the newspaper?

Wives' Chorus: Sure we do.

Me: Then you're not spending every waking moment with your precious children. I'll bet you send them out to the yard or into their rooms to play when you're busy. I'll bet you tell them to keep quiet when you're on the telephone. I'll bet you deposit them at other children's homes—not just to expand their acquaintanceships but to ensure yourself free time. I'll just bet that none of you spend any more uninterrupted time with your children than a working mother like me does.

Wife C: Ridiculous! I always watch my children play. I talk with them, play with them, sit with them at lunch.

Me: Sounds very busy. And what does your husband do with them when he gets home?

Wife C: Oh, they're asleep by the time he gets home. Come six o'clock I can't *wait* to get them into bed.

If that's a loving mother, I'm a Lebanese juggler.

The circle of wives mumbled disclaimers and murmured in discomfort. One of their number had betrayed them. Was the lid off the Pandora's box of trapped, sterile harassed house-wifehood? Is each day only to be endured with one's children until they can be packed off to bed? Are these women fulfilling a role compulsively and without enjoyment?

I don't think so. Probably, their defensiveness escalated their assault. This group of women overreacted to me as a challenge to their own status. I don't really believe that all of them suffer through endless days of demanding children and bleak house-hold duties.

Harassed housewives vs. happy homemakers

Many women are sincerely gratified by full-time motherhood. I know only a few of them but I do know one such woman intimately. My sister, Betty, thrives on the smooth operation of her home and the busy interaction between the parents and four children in the family. Her home is very much a career to her. She runs it enthusiastically, efficiently and with utter devotion. She's a cheerful, professional homemaker. Women's magazines and home-furnishing brochures are her trade papers. Her kitchen shelf contains dozens of file folders that would put some offices to shame. (In answer to two of my current needs, Betty recently presented me with her files on "Children's Parties" and "How to Add a Powder Room." Do *you* know how to make finger paints out of corn starch or how to fit a bathroom into forty-nine inches of space?) Because my sister *chose* to be a full-time homemaker she suffered no frustrated hindsight of what she might have been. Reading, community affairs, involvement with her husband's work in education administration gave her complete satisfaction apart from the stimulation she found in the home.

Betty went back to teaching a few years ago when her youngest child was well along in school. She's glad to be out in the world again, but she looks back on her stay-at-home years with the absolute conviction that they constituted a rich, full life.

For her and others like her, work is something you do before your children arrive and after they've grown up. This book isn't really talking to them. Because to them a career will always be a man's thing—like the Army or power tools.

What I mean to illustrate with the scene at the New Year's

Eve party is the complex ambivalence that a great many women feel about working. They're the ones who chose to abandon careers or never to start them and they never feel quite right about that decision. They regret their choice but feel bound by it. They may be mildly discontented or terribly bitter but somehow they haven't gotten around to correcting the situation. Some tell themselves that they aren't equipped to "do" anything now that ten years have elapsed since they last worked or attended school. Others excuse their inertia by claiming that their children would never stand for it. Still more swear that they are shackled by a husband who insists that a woman's place is at the stove and at his service.

As I see it, a woman who desires no different life than the one she leads would not feel impelled to attack the life style of the working wife and mother. She would not need to undermine another woman's confidence in order to enhance her own.

The ones on the attack, I believe to be acting out of defensiveness. They would really like to be doing something. But for their separate reasons they aren't. So they seek to reinforce their positions by finding fault with mine. If I were to crumble in a heap of self-doubt and guilt they could be reassured that their road was the right one.

After the New Year was ushered in and the champagne floated the party into the wee hours, it came to light that one of my questioners had been a scientist and intended to go back into research. Another wife had just taken an interview for a job as a part-time physical therapist. A third woman planned to work as a technical writer when her child started school.

I became more convinced than ever that many educated women feel stymied by household chores. They are stultified by constant child care and children's company. Not all women. But some.

Why do they perpetuate the myth of Woman Equals Mother/

Wife? I've told you my theory. There are two culprits: women who want to justify their own martyred, self-sacrificing position and men who want to keep the status quo as comfy cozy as it's always been.

The feminists may be on to something

I'm not obsessed with the problem. And I'm not the crusading type. For myself, my own adjustment to being a working mother is right for me. I'm not hell-bent on converting every house-wife I meet at a party. But there are banner-waving feminists around and their view of the situation—though extreme—is worth some attention. One such group is the National Organization for Women whose credo is "Full equality for all women in America in truly equal partnership with men."

They argue that masculine prejudice, custom and statutory law have conspired to keep women in the home or in minor jobs at low salaries. The NOW literature makes quite a case for the slavery of sexuality. They say "women are not valued for their intelligence but only as wives and mothers which, stripping the matter of its traditional sacred cows, reduced the Woman's Role to a sort of socially acceptable whoredom."

It's a topsy-turvy world where a female engineer for General Dynamics can be fired from her $18,000-a-year job because she refused to wear a bra and urged a "braless Friday" for the 2200 girls at the plant (she's suing for $1.4 million); where a Mississippi penitentiary permits married male prisoners con-jugal visiting by their wives but denies the same rights to married women prisoners; where prostitution laws punish the female for selling her body but not the male who patronizes her; where training programs for college graduates feed males into the management pool and females into the secretarial pool (though they could sink or swim at the low end of the salary scale with or without the training program); where a married woman who has worked all her life often draws lower social security benefits than the wife, widow or even divorcée who has never held a job but who is compensated as a dependent of her retired husband.

As long as these kinds of infuriating inequalities exist, we are fortunate that the revolutionary feminist groups are stirring up the troubled waters for all of us. We need them to serve as the conscience for our male-oriented society and as lobbyists in the political arena where progress can be measured in concrete legal reforms.

Speaking for the woman whose house is just a home, not a way of life, NOW demands such liberating innovations as a full tax deduction of housekeeping and child-care expenses for working parents, a paid maternity leave and a guarantee for a woman's right to return to her job after childbirth, a nationwide network of child-care centers operating as optional community facilities and a constitutional amendment withholding federal funds from any agency, institution or organization discriminating against women.

These are not unreasonable requests. They're great ideas. They have been largely ignored for many reasons. The problem doesn't seem pressing to politicians and policy makers. People are offended by the strident attitude assumed by feminists. Men tend to react to these requests as they reacted to the suffragette's demands in the early part of this century. They dismiss these demanding ladies as the lunatic fringe and respond to the whole movement only with ridicule.

It's too bad that our society has made so little progress in freeing talented, aspiring women from their homes. It accounts for a tremendous waste of human potential. It causes frustration in women who value their abilities and tension in marriages where one partner feels unfulfilled. It accounts for the sad statistics cited by the National Organization for Women: of the twenty-eight million women in the job market, seventy-five per cent of them are in rock-bottom positions, ninety per cent of them earn less than $5000 a year and many of them earn up to forty per cent less than men who hold the exact same jobs.

Behind the statistics covering women in general is an important subcategory. The working wife and mother is subject to all the disadvantages common to any female looking for a job plus a whole host of special pressures and societal excuses. She is perhaps the aspirant with the most strikes against her and the most doors slammed in her face.

I could spit nails when I hear the usual condescending "explanations" for employers' dense stubbornness. There *are* answers to every allegation. The enlightened employer has discovered them for himself. The company or industry or boss who would try them on me would get a lot of back talk.

"You won't be free to travel."

To this I say, partly right, partly wrong. I'm not applying for a job as a traveling salesman. If the job I do want involves constant travel, then tell me and I'll bow out. Sure, I don't care to leave my family regularly or for weeks on end. But if what you mean is an occasional overnight out-of-town conference, a weekend convention or a week abroad once every two years, just try me. If my husband and I agree that I would be happiest working, we are also implicitly in agreement that some of my duties will cause us inconvenience—like my occasional absence from home. If I take a job with full knowledge that traveling or late hours or occasional weekend work is involved, you may be sure that I'll be as faithful to my obligations as a single man who hasn't a responsibility in the world.

"You don't need the raise because you've got a husband supporting you."

Wrong. I need the raise because I deserve the raise; because in our system merit is rewarded in money; because I justify the economics of my working on the balance sheet between my income and such expenses as transportation, baby-sitters, wardrobe and lunches. I need the raise because I know that if I were a man or if I were working here without your knowing my biographical facts, I would get that raise.

"How can I be sure you'll stay?"

You can't. But neither can you be sure that any man you hire will stay. The average man stays with the same employer only four years. His reasons for moving on are probably the same as mine would be: to get a better job elsewhere. Once I am a working wife or mother I have established my desire to remain in the business world. *You* must assume that once in I'm here to stay.

"You're just working for fun and extra money."

Maybe I am. But so what? Finding fun and gaining extra money are in themselves a pretty strong incentive for succeeding in business. In fact, if I'm so clearly applying here by choice and not out of need, shouldn't you be more confident of my having a good attitude?

But maybe I'm not. Maybe the fun and extra money are just ancillary benefits. Maybe I have the same motivations common to other applicants. Maybe I really want the job, like the work and can do it exceedingly well. Maybe, just maybe, I am extraordinarily endowed with the ubiquitous talent to be my husband's lover, a good cook, a creative mother, an able housekeeper *and* a fantastic copywriter on your staff. Maybe you should think of what we have in common—a brain—instead of what differentiates us—my family responsibilities.

"We can't spare the time you'll need to take off for P.T.A. conferences or for your child's bout with German measles."

Just tell me your limit on sick days and don't second guess me on my absences. I may be absent because my child is having his tonsils out but I won't take off to fulfill my obligations at Army Reserve meetings. I might take a morning for a teacher's conference at school but I won't be out with a hangover. You don't give your male applicants a warning in advance. You don't grill them to discover if they lift weights and therefore may end up out of the office with a hernia. Don't anticipate. Just tell me the company rules and I'll abide by them.

"We want people whose first loyalty is to their jobs."

Come now. Are you telling me that your own wife and five kids don't come first? Why should a woman be any less able to split her energies than a man is? Why don't we call you "Working Fathers?" Because it's understood by sensible people that you can shoulder both lives without collapsing. Your wife can be suffering postpartum blues, your son can be palling around with a drug-taking crowd, your car payments can be two months overdue and the cesspool can have overflowed the night before—you'll still manage to get through the business day in a passable state of productivity. No one presents you with either/or loyalties. Naturally I'm going to love my husband and children a zillion times more than I love my job. So do you, I hope. Certainly, if it's a question of success on the job or the health and well-being of my family, I'd tell the job to go to hell. Wouldn't you?

"It's a $95 a week, take it or leave it. And you'd be smart to take it."

You take it. I'll leave it. If I know that the assistant art director down the hall is making $150 a week and that the person who held the job up until now was making $150 a week, I want $150 a week. If I'm worth hiring, I'm worth paying the going rate. Fifty-five dollars is a stiff handicap for an applicant who happens to have a husband and a child or two. I may not be the hottest commodity in the job market place but neither am I marked-down merchandise.

Big boss man will be watching

The woman who encounters resistance such as this and talks her way into a desirable job deserves a pat on the back and a generous dose of sympathy. She'll be under surveillance for weeks and maybe months. If she's a working wife, her employer will watch for signs of morning sickness and a euphoric look that may signal the beginning of a pregnancy and the end of her job. If she's already a mother, he'll be keeping close tabs on her attendance record and her phone calls. After six months of punctuality, he'll pounce on her the day she leaves the office at five minutes to five because she had to get her son to the dentist by five-fifteen. Those are the breaks. Discriminatory attitudes die hard. But there does eventually come a day when the quality of a woman's work overshadows her marital or maternal status.

Girls who, like myself, undergo the metamorphosis from single girl to married woman to mother while on the same job have it much easier for this very reason. The boss and the company know what the woman can do. A rational man does not expect a woman to cease being an effective executive the minute she returns from her honeymoon. A fair-minded boss doesn't fear for the safety of the accounting department simply because the chief comptroller is seven months pregnant. And a survey taker is not thought to have lost her touch after a six-week maternity leave.

That is not to say that crucial changes in a woman's personal life do not affect her. They do. But for the most part, changes for the better in one's basic life status—getting married, or having children—are monumentally favorable changes. They tend to distract a girl, of course. However, the daydreaming, engaged girl soon becomes a contented wife and the euphoric pregnant woman relaxes quickly enough into the satisfactions of real motherhood. Taking it one step further, you have the simple syllogism: women are most content when they are happy wives and satisfied mothers. Female executives are women. Therefore, female executives who are happy wives and satisfied mothers are the most content.

Everyone knows that contented cows give the richest milk. So, too, contented women in business do the best work!

These truths seem so self-evident. It's a wonder that working wives and mothers ever have to defend or explain their positions. But we do. Very recently I interviewed a television producer who has frequently worked with female colleagues. He was full of kudos for the quality of the women's work and the extent of their talent. He praised their dedication and their professionalism. He even said that two women he knew in television were better at their jobs than any men he could think of and still they were thoroughly feminine.

Eureka! I thought I had discovered a true equalitarian. But when I asked him to comment on working *wives* he had known, a subtle note of condemnation crept into his voice.

"I'm always a little suspicious of a woman who is successful after marriage," he said. "Why should she have the same drive afterward? Her ego should be completely satisfied once she has a husband."

"Rubbish," said I, totally abandoning my interviewing objectivity. "You have a good marriage. But *your* ego hasn't shut up shop."

"A man doesn't live only through his marriage. A man has a stake in the larger world," he answered.

"Then why doesn't your excellent golf game or your terrific bridge score or your superb understanding of the Cold War do enough to satisfy your ego?" I challenged.

"I suppose a man's ego requirements are more varied. For example, my wife is totally absorbed in cooking and fussing around our house. She called me out of a production meeting this morning to remind me to buy a head of lettuce on my way home. I find this charming and I approve," he smiled.

"Great. If she can find fulfillment in planning the salad at ten o'clock in the morning, I approve too," I said. "But will you allow that all women are not like your wife in that respect? We may also think about the lettuce. But we're likely to sandwich that thought in between a budget meeting and a violent reaction to a New York *Times* editorial.

"Working wives can also have wifely natures. I, too, have called my husband out of meetings."

"For what?" he asked.

"For four reasons," I replied. "To discuss the bombing halt. To ask him to buy a hundred shares of a new stock issue. To read him my advertising copy. And to ask him to bring home a head of lettuce."

So much for roughage. And so much for the rough stuff dealt out to working wives and mothers. It's really only a matter of time before we become a totally accepted segment of the job corps. The financial columnist Sylvia Porter reports that one in three married women in the United States are now in the labor force and the proportion is rising steadily. Already, rock-ribbed policies and practices are changing to accommodate us. Miss Porter lists some of the most encouraging ones currently in effect at progressive companies. One allows the working mother time off with pay to take her children for periodic doctor's visits. (A wise move and one not as altruistic as it sounds. A healthy child will not require its mother at home beside the sick bed.) Another firm pays part of a girl's dental bills and those of her spouse and offspring. Life insurance covering the employee's entire family is becoming common. And some companies provide attractive educational benefits for the staffer and college scholar-ships for her kids. There's even one employer who offers a pa-ternity leave for new fathers in addition to a standard six-week maternity leave. (Now, *there's* equalitarianism at its ultimate.)

Never underestimate the power of a working woman and a willing employer

Working wives who have no strong union doing battle for them and those who find little elasticity in their management will have to break new ground. It takes only a willing boss and a workable arrangement the first time around to convert management to make wholesale policy revisions.

A gal who works in educational television likes to travel with her husband, who is an importer. The husband had to go to Scandinavia for three weeks. The working wife had already used up her vacation time during the past summer. Unfortu-nately, the TV station severely frowns on those who want to take off time without pay. So, to take the sting out of her request for time off without pay—and to ensure that her job was still there when she returned—she made a deal. She checked to see if any of the station's film projects had anything at all to do with Europe. She found that there was a film in progress on the twentieth anniversary of V-E Day and the international reac-tion of the man-in-the-street to the formal end of the war in Europe. She asked the film's producers what footage they had to illustrate the event and what, ideally, they should have but didn't. They had stuff on Admiral Doenitz's announcement of Hitler's death and they had film of the fall of Berlin. But they would dearly love to show something of the German surrender in Italy, the Netherlands and Denmark.

Aha! Denmark was one of the countries my friend's husband

had to visit. The girl offered to spend a good portion of her time in Denmark seeking out private film collections, municipal archives and other film repositories. She suggested that she interview Danish citizens who had lived through the occupation and who had sharp memories of V-E Day. She promised to hunt for still pictures, documents, wartime mementos—anything that would serve as a visual contribution to the film special.

The producers were naturally delighted to have a volunteer. Educational TV is not known for its generous travel budgets. Here they were getting a willing researcher for nothing. They prevailed upon the girl's superiors to let her take the three weeks without pay, to travel with her husband and just possibly —no guarantees—bring back some valuable historical material.

The girl did just what she promised and had a marvelous experience in the process. She was with her husband when he was free from his business and she was gainfully occupied as a historical sleuth when he was tied up. She returned loaded down with material. She found her job *and* a sizable raise awaiting her.

Never underestimate the power of a working wife. With a constructive imagination, a taste for setting new precedents and a well-developed power of persuasion, she can help teach rigid businessmen an important lesson. *Just because something has never been done doesn't mean it won't work.*

Everything that my boss and I devised to keep us both happy *has* worked. And much of it had never been done before. Before my children were born, there were actually few instances when an adjustment or compromise had to be made. Obviously, a woman with no children has no special demands made upon her time and energies during the workday. Her husband is also presumably holding down a job that keeps him occupied from nine to five or thereabouts. I used to talk to my husband once a day and occasionally meet him for lunch—no more of a diversion from the job than a man or a single woman might have.

Still, my boss made enough gestures that indicated to me that he was very much aware of my new marriage. I remember once in the early months when Mr. Geis overheard me asking one of the girls for a recipe suggestion. He came into my office five minutes later with one of the cookbooks from his library of other publishers' books. When Mr. Geis heard that my husband had won one of his most important cases I was given the rest of the day off. My boss gave me a guest voucher for two dinners that night at one of New York's best restaurants—a celebration meal on him.

Now, there's something that had never been done. But it worked as well as if it had initiated an official reciprocal trade agreement. Subsequently, if my boss needed me to stay late or to take a visiting foreign agent to dinner, my husband never had a beef. Bert doesn't complain (very much) when we drink ourselves blind at the airport waiting for an author on a flight that's six hours late on the very night when Bert wanted to see the Knick's game. You give a little, you get a little.

It was an easy, fair and square give-and-take when I was simply a working wife. Once I became a working mother the plot thickened. It would be safe to say that it was still give-and-take. I gave a lot of trouble and Mr. Geis kindly took it. Our particular adjustment has been so ideal, quite frankly, because of his gambling spirit. He has been a consistent proponent of the "Let's try it" philosophy.

I quit "for good" at the end of my first pregnancy. I was convinced at that time that I was meant to be a full-time mother. (See how close I came to being one of those frustrated stay-at-homes!) My boss was convinced that I'd be back. He held the job open. Six months later I was back.

When our third baby was born, Mr. Geis was wishing for a

boy even more than we were. After twin girls he felt that the birth of a boy would halt my procreation by satisfying my craving for a well-balanced family and Bert's need for an heir. When the boss was in England he saluted me with this cablegram: "HOPE YOUR YOUNGEST WILL BE A BOY AND LONG MAY HE BE YOUR YOUNGEST." It had continued to be a standing joke between us that I might retire again for six months. This time, however, I had only a six-week-paid maternity leave. When I was feeling up to it, my secretary brought paperwork to my home and I sent work back to the office by messenger. The office health-insurance policy paid the hospital bills.

Creative motherhood

Being a working mother does not interfere with my personal goals where creative motherhood is concerned. Because I have a baby-sitter who is also a housekeeper, I am able to ignore major cleaning chores on at-home days. My husband and I try to plan activities that are enjoyable for all of us and often educational to the kids. In our family, we've dubbed such activities "adventures." This can encompass something so seemingly modest as a ride on the bus or subway (a colossal adventure to a three-year-old), to a walk along the waterfront waving at the tugboats, to a full-fledged outing including a visit to the zoo or museum, perhaps a Chinese tea-lunch, a stop in the playground, ice skating or an indulgent jaunt through a toy store. On rainy days we may make papier-mâché candleholders or greeting cards for the holidays or my husband may construct complex cities out of blocks, chessmen and anything wee and wondrous that happens to be around the house.

As I said before, it isn't how much time you spend with your

children but how well you spend it. The important thing is to
make the time a total involvement—a family adventure.

Let's suppose you're confronted with the dilemma of giving
up your job in favor of your children but you suspect that it
shouldn't even be a dilemma. In the long run, you realize that
you'll be a better mother if you're happy. And your work makes
you happy. No sweat—or only a little. First and foremost in this
situation is the complete approval of your husband. Second, and
in its way just as important, is your choice of baby-sitter or
housekeeper. You must trust her as you do yourself. If you don't
have complete confidence in her judgment or if you doubt, in
the slightest, her ability to love your kids and give them full,
warm attention—then stay home until you find the right woman.
No job, however fantastic, is worth risking a child's psychological
and physical well-being. You should hire someone who understands that the children come first. The house can look like hell,
the wash can pile up, eggs can be curdling in the Hollandaise
but if the baby is crying, she must hold it, comfort it and
minister to its discontent.

If you have school-age children, your concern will obviously
lessen. Their hours at home before you return from the office
will be minimal. Nevertheless, it's the nine-year-old who decides to experiment with a match so that he can play fireman.
And he can get into as much trouble between 3:30 and 5:30
as the ten-month-old who crawls around the iron cord at eleven
in the morning.

The mother who works has an added challenge. The precious
hours she does spend with her family are compensatory. She
will want to use them to make up for her time away from
home. She won't spend an hour putting on her face in the
morning. She'll use that hour to talk to an eight-year-old about
his pitching arm. Or she'll spend it stringing wooden beads
with a toddler. She won't dash in at 6 P.M. and immediately

get on the telephone with a friend while the child waits for her attention. She'll perhaps order naps for the youngest children so that they'll be able to stay up to be with Mommy and Daddy for a few hours in the evening. If the office is nearby, she'll come home for lunch occasionally. And she'll use weekends for those adventures we talked about. With Daddy along on the weekend adventures to a play, picnic, long walk or family day at home, a child will never feel cheated.

By the same token, the working mother will not feel guilty about leading her double life. The point is, such a life *can* be led if you feel it's for you and you are willing to apportion your time with infinite care and judicious advance planning.

Going back to work

Are you listening, unrequited stay-at-homes? Why not subject your daily life to some relentless scrutiny? You, too, can pick up the threads no matter how long ago you left the man's world for the world of washer-dryer repairmen. Put yourself in the hands of a good employment agent and just see what plums you might be offered. A lady editor in my company went back into the fray after nearly ten years of housewifery. She had taken a few dozen free-lance editing assignments through the years but she still felt frightfully out of touch. Imagine her delight when she had no difficulty getting a job and, better still, when she realized that editing techniques hadn't changed in ten years. Of course they hadn't. And unless you are a refugee from some job which is now performed entirely by computer, you too will probably fit right back into the niche.

Even if you never had a niche or if you are no longer thrilled by the field for which you were originally trained, there's a certain excitement about starting something brand-new.

Wouldn't it be fun to forget that you're forty-one and to start fresh on the career climb along with the twenty-one-year-olds? As I've said many times before, there's room for all of us. And part time or full time, there's room for you. So hang up your apron, have your hair done and start reading those want ads.

Life is as full as you choose to make it. Our old friend Brendan Behan used to make up "Least Likely" axioms, which were wry, negative statements of truth. The most famous of these was: "A city is a place where you are least likely to get bitten by a wild sheep." But my favorite Least Likely which is most applicable here was: "A man who has nothing to do is a man who is least likely to have time to do anything." The same, and more, holds true for a woman.

I have two friends who don't work in offices. One has trouble maintaining the status quo in her five-room apartment. She can barely get the beds made, the children's meals on the table, her husband's dinner done and the kitchen cleaned up between eight in the morning and twelve midnight. She's a musician who hasn't touched her concert grand piano in half a year.

The other stay-at-home lady has three kids and a large house. It's always spotless. The meals are gourmet delights. Even the kids lunch on stuffed avocados and homemade éclairs. The woman is an author and illustrator of children's books. She turns out two or three a year. She also makes elegant tapestries, does collages out of bits of jewels, fabrics and buttons, is active in the P.T.A. and does seemingly dozens of fantastic things for the community. Same number of hours in the day. Same number of children. Same basic chores. One girl is barely getting by, the other is gilding her life with rewarding accomplishments.

Another duo for purposes of comparison. Both working mothers are composites of recognizable types. The first woman leaves for the office before her kids have even dressed for school. She works a full week. Her children eat at 6 P.M. She doesn't get home before seven and usually it's closer to eight. Sometimes the children are in bed when she arrives and for days in a row she actually sees them just to say hello. Her husband follows his own schedule. Often he is fed dinner by the maid. They seem to meet only for cocktails on weekends. She reads trade journals in bed at night. Never seems able to catch up with her work. Sends the maid to Open School Day to check on the kids' progress. Hasn't cooked a meal herself, mended a sock, read a book other than a required business text or met her children's best friends. She knows she falls short as a mother but she can't possibly juggle the job and the home from Monday through Friday. On the weekends she rests up by entertaining business associates, watching some escapist television and sleeping a lot. She figures she'll work until she's forty and then she'll quit and catch up with the family.

They may not be there when she's ready for them. And she may not have much to show for her single-minded devotion to her career.

The other working mother manages to touch base in both home and company and score in both places. She never fails to have breakfast with her family. She comes home and cooks dinner for the family on most weekday nights and everyone eats at the same time. She and her husband play tennis every Thursday night at an indoor court. She reads a newspaper every day and is often into two books at once. She sculpts in a room which also serves as a children's playroom. So she's near her sons even when involved with her hobby. She's an expert Italian cook and her husband loves her meals. One night a week, after her boys are in bed, she catches up on architectural publications. She has her architectural equipment in the basement. If the work load demands it, she brings her drawings home. She often takes her family to watch the construction of houses and stores that she has designed. She sews her own clothes.

The examples speak for themselves. Most of us could be completely in control of our life styles. The children's book author and the architect haven't got a patent on the thirty-hour day. They know how to fill their time in such a way that satisfaction and achievement are the natural rewards of nearly every activity. Time is our unsung natural resource. It's sort of like the atom. Until it was split there was no such thing as atomic energy. All that energy locked up in the atom like a secret is not so different from the personal energy and explosive talent which goes undiscovered, locked up in a block of wasted time.

Having your cake and making it too

Women who are able to split their time to serve all the complex needs and commitments that matter to them are often working wives and mothers. With one foot firmly planted in the business world and the other foot sliding around on a loose marble or a waxed floor in the home, this multipurpose female is a stranger to boredom. She reads *Aviation Week & Space Technology* under the hair dryer and grows chives in her office window "because it gets more sun than at home." She can discourse for hours on rising interest rates but she's always the one woman in a crowd who has a foolproof method of separating egg yolks—"use your hands." She can recite in sequence the dates of her product's spring advertising campaign, her dinner party for twelve, her daughter's next visit to the orthodontist and her secretary's birthday—without benefit of calendar. She knows by heart her Diners' Card number, her son's locker combination and her husband's Social Security number. She translates her penchant for organization and efficiency to her home, keeping impeccable recipe files, tax records and stock market lists in the file cabinet under her dressing table.

This Compleat Woman is not a myth. She exists by the thousands. Her secret of success is easy to emulate up to a point. You *can* retrain yourself to use time more profitably. You *can* learn to regiment yourself so that you never shortchange either job or home. You *can*, with luck, convert your company or convince your boss to let you try an unconventional working arrangement. But here the molding, shaping and cajoling come to a halt. It ain't worth a damn if you ain't got that man—the right man who understands what will make you happy and who recognizes your potential as a separate individual.

That's really the crux of the matter. Making it in marriage, motherhood *and* the market place requires first that you're making it in your marriage. You should be sure that your husband adores you, that he's proud of your performance in your profession and that he approves of your techniques of leading a double life. It helps if he honestly enjoys hearing about the kind of work you do and if he happens to be compatible with your business friends and associates.

There may have been a few reader dropouts in this chapter— girls who feel marriage is a remote possibility at this stage of life; girls who are really only working to bide their time until Prince Charming spirits them away to Palm Springs or Perth Amboy; girls who marry implacable old-fashioned husbands ("A woman's place is in the home—and no back talk") and presumably the poor girls were forewarned about this attitude before they married; girls who marry surveyors in Tasmania, forest rangers in Millinocket, Maine or Peace Corps administrators in Bengal (these gals have new worlds to conquer at their husband's sides).

But for the rest of us, Onward and Upward with the Occupation is the keynote after marriage, with a loving husband's consent and commiseration. You don't have to be schizoid. Both lives can mesh beautifully and enhance each other in the process. You can move from the office swivel chair to the living-room love seat to the baby's high chair without missing a beat. And without missing any of the infinite variations of pleasure and fulfillment that the combined worlds can provide.

You become more pleasant and productive on the job when your private life is secure, when you're happy and settled with the man you love. And vice versa. You are a more interesting wife when you bring home some of the excitement of your profession. You have something substantial to share or contribute to those pleasant hours of conversation that keep a marriage alive. Your husband can join with you in the ancillary activities of your job, just as you do in his. You make friends with each other's friends.

There are those who are satisfied to see themselves solely as the offshoot of the man they married. I know many women who thrive on living vicariously through their husbands and children. The wife gains status and identity because her husband is known to be a brilliant doctor or a highly successful merchant. She becomes *persona grata* in her community and in her own mind because she has beautiful or remarkably intelligent children or because hers is the biggest house in the neighborhood. One can make a fair comparison with the socialite surviving on faded class credentials. Now even baronesses, Rockefellers and Vanderbilts have ceased resting on the laurels of their bloodline. They don't *have* to use their talents or expend their personal energies, but they do. Why so many wives still hide behind their husbands' and children's credentials strikes me as the anachronism of the age of emancipation.

One has only to read the daily lovelorn columns or the monthly "How to Save Your Marriage" articles to know that connubial bliss is more often connubial hit or miss. A recent marriage quiz unearthed such common complaints as boredom, a lack of things in common, mundane conversation or total silence and a lack of respect between partners. Separation was the keynote of relationships where neither husband nor wife had ever entertained the thought of formal legal separation. A bleak picture of gradual psychological, emotional, intellectual and eventually physical separation emerged from the questionnaires. One wife admitted that she couldn't "stand the sound of her husband's key in the lock every night." A businessman said he was too ashamed of his wife's "ignorance and her dowdy appearance to ever take her out in public."

There are convoluted explanations for deep breakdowns of the marital relationship which only an expert can fully probe. But there seemed to be an immediate, superficial correlation with the factors of early marriage, extreme divergence in educational background *and* what the wife does all day.

While husbands are always moving, changing, developing and expanding in the outside world they prowl every business day, their stay-at-home wives become more insulated and stagnant as the years pass.

In contrast, the working wife seems able to give as good as she gets: to offer an enthusiastic, self-actualized personality to the marriage; to have a "self" in the same sense that her husband does.

Less important but just as real is the fact that the working wife is likely to maintain her appearance. At the tenth reunion of my husband's law school graduating class, you could pick out the working wives by the shortness of their hems, the casualness of their hair styles and the trimness of their figures. How appealing is an attractive wife? Ask the man who has one. Or, better still, ask the man who doesn't.

Nobody's naïve enough to suggest that your man married you for the job you hold. But if he pursued, wooed and won you while you were a single woman working at that job, it's safe to assume that part of the you that he loves is the you that loves your work. He may not want you to quit. He may love the fresh, new dimension it brings into *his* life.

I can only speak authoritatively about my own experience. My husband and I have a rare symbiosis in that deep down in my heart I would like to be a labor lawyer and deep down in his lurks a book publisher yearning to get out. Bert plays an integral role in the man's world that I occupy. He loves to attend National Book Awards ceremonies, trade cocktail parties, interesting television bookings and dinners with authors like Groucho Marx (no, Groucho doesn't always crouch over, chomp on a cigar and chase girls) or Jacqueline Susann. Because he is a lawyer he is especially interested in our publishing contracts. He sweats out our knotty negotiations and contributes free legal advice during our occasional bouts of litigation. He has attended copyright workshops with me. He has been to Authors League receptions and to motion-picture screenings. He's always coming up with book ideas, publicity suggestions and reliable reactions to my brainstorms (remember Scarsdale Research?). I've been to lawyers' lectures, clients' homes and top level meetings. I kibbitz, read all his briefs and know the details of all his cases.

The symbiotic relationship was never more apparent than at a recent dinner party. On one side of the table I was regaling my companions with triumphant reports about Bert's prowess at settling a school strike. On the other side of the table he was describing a publicity gimmick I dreamed up. Later in the evening when everyone was talking about children, Bert volunteered a quote from our four-year-old, Robin ("I'm starving tired!") and I contributed one of Abigail's *bon mots* ("My chest doesn't breast right"). There in microcosm is the best illustration of my point of view. Instead of the woman talking only house and kids and the man talking only business, there was six-way cross-pollination. It all adds up to a lot of shared interests, mutual respect and enormous pride in one another.

Without Bert's approval and encouragement I'm sure I would not have resumed my career. But I can't say I would have been as zestful a wife and mother if I hadn't. For me, each segment of life nourishes the other. Eight or ten hours of pressurized telephone work one day at the office . . . the next day home to a toy telephone and a fantasy conversation with the man-in-the-moon or Little Miss Muffet. A dressed-up week at the office gives me a taste for a weekend in blue jeans. A week devoted to planning a twelve-city promotion tour for an author may inspire me to spend an evening planning an imaginative vacation for our family. After Friday's crises in the office or peregrinations to and from TV studios, I'm delighted to spend Saturday in the garden, walking with the family through Greenwich Village or attending a stellar performance of *Peter and the Wolf.*

So the big question is Why Not Do Both? You may answer, "O.K. I'm with you on *both.* Work and wifehood. But when baby makes three the picture becomes 3-D."

Agreed, of course. Children complicate matters. But if you're a mother by choice and a working woman by preference, both decisions can be compatible if they lead to happiness for you. Happiness is self-nourishing. A pleased, gratified woman is a pleasure-giving mother. The choice should be yours on both issues.

When to have children

I have some thoughts on family planning that even Margaret Sanger never thought of. It is now commonly accepted that one has children when good and ready. It has also become respectable to plan children to fit into your economic situation. Why

then shouldn't a woman plan her children to fit into her personal and professional life as well as her husband's?

Many cling to the sentiment "Children Come First." They
mean literally. To these true believers it is cold and unfeeling
to suggest that a couple might first want a round-the-world tour
before child-rearing years begin in earnest. Parents may want a
few carefree, child-free years to enjoy each other. They may
want to launch a crash campaign to stow away a nest egg.
Should such couples feel like selfish ogres? Hell, no. The marriage comes first!

In the same spirit, I don't think it's barbaric to take into consideration the demands of a job when planning one's family. We
wanted children fairly early in our marriage. But we were also
set on having one full year—a winter and a summer as un-
encumbered newlyweds.

Friends of ours put off having kids until the husband *and*
wife could find good jobs in the Midwest because they were
adamant about not raising a child on the streets of New York.

Another couple time their children's births so that the wife is
never pregnant during the best months of the ski season.

One always hears about people who try to have their children
born in December so that they can get a full $600 deduction
for the whole tax year.

Different reasons for timing children strike different people
as eminently logical. For us, it's a combination of several factors,
not the least of which are the demands of my job. I wasn't the
least bit surprised when Jacqueline Susann asked me when
Bert and I intended to have our next child. At that time my
company had Jackie's second novel, *The Love Machine*, under
contract and tentatively scheduled for publication in the spring
of 1969. Jackie and I had worked well together and I didn't
think it odd for her to wonder whether I might be off on maternity leave just when her publicity campaign would be in full

flower. I reassured her that we hoped to have our third child in the spring of 1968 and I wasn't the tiniest bit insulted by her invasion of our privacy.

My second pregnancy was completely premeditated. We wanted a three-year separation between the girls and the new baby. We wanted a trip to Europe while I was still thin and mobile. We figured that writing this book during those nine months would fit in with the doctor's prescription for sedentary activity. And finally, I would again have my maternity leave during the summer months which are the slowest in the publishing industry. Calculating? Yes—but not in a way that hurts anybody. These plans were only calculated to be best for Bert and me and our needs. And since life is such a chancy thing anyway, why not exercise what little intelligent control we can over it?

Children are most welcome, most cherished and best loved when the parents feel that no self-sacrifices were involved in their births. One of the most treacherous games people play is "If it weren't for you . . ." Frequently it is a woman who plays that game with the child whose arrival interfered with some other desire. Our children are not burdens, substitutes or accidents—they are precious additions to our life.

The best man

You can plan the arrival of your children a lot more readily than you can plan the advent of the right husband. If you're single, successful and having a wonderful time, more power to you. But if the Miss in front of your name is becoming as much a part of your identity as your name itself, then beware. Singlehood, especially for the successful lady executive, can become habit-forming. The girl who is hooked on business fame and fortune marries her job and uses her subordinates as offspring.

Even those who avoid this pitfall often discover they are substituting business projects for babies. A career can never be a
stand-in for the rich, full life.

For all your unpsyched-up *joie de vivre* on the job, let's face
facts. The world moves in twos. Marriage, besides its private
joys, lets you into that warm, comfortable cocoon of married
couples—a world that operates quite apart from any other, no
matter what field you're in. Big-time business functions are man-
and-wife deals. Having a charming husband is almost as much
an asset in business as it is to you personally. But unless he's
the kind of guy who will

> pick you up at the office because your briefcase is too
> heavily loaded and your shoes pinch,
>
> foot the bill for the most competent baby-sitter that money
> can buy,
>
> get up at 4 A.M. to give a relief bottle even though you
> both have to work the next day,
>
> take the kids out for a whole Sunday so that you can catch
> up on your work,
>
> treat you to a restaurant dinner because you're too pooped
> to cook,

unless he can be counted on for such superhusband service,
think twice about leading your double life. It can't possibly be
pulled off by you alone. *He's* got to be with you every step of
the way. That's what can make it work effortlessly.

If he's a smart, witty, masculine, understanding, marvelous
husband (like mine), his very existence is a virtual guarantee
that everything will come up roses no matter where you sow
the seeds of your career. If the signs are right, sow them. Don't
just bury them deep in the fertile garden of your husband's

accomplishments. Don't keep them in their seed packet locked up in the kitchen drawer after marriage. Roses need light and air.

Before I succumb to rose fever from this runaway metaphor, I'd better state my druthers on the whole subject of marriage, motherhood and the market place—and call it a chapter. It's better to be satisfied than frustrated; it's better to be working than not working; it's better to be married than single; it's better to be a mommy as well as a Mrs. But it's *best* to be all four at once!

10.

But what about the real me?

*I*t's a good question. And a pointed one in an age when Freud is dragged into all the fun. What about the real you? Who is she? Are you sure that there *is* a real you? Is she distinct from some other you that operates in the practical situations of daily life? Could it be that this essence, this ultimate identity contains no more "youness" than the you who makes coffee in the morning, gets dressed, takes a bus to the office and puts in eight hours in some field of commerce?

A little introspection goes a long way. All of us have indulged in "soul-searching" sessions—alone on a beach or in a huddle of girls in a school dormitory. Enlightenment comes in many forms. Most of our most crucial moments of self-discovery result from private questioning and brutal self-analysis. Sometimes we are greatly affected by readings in philosophy or psychology or by a random inspirational book. We change because of things our friends say about us. Some of us seek professional therapy. Others "drop out" of society when they find no "meaning" in it and no place in its structure.

It all amounts to the same thing: who am I? This book has not been concerned with the final answer to that question. It has not been intended in any sense as a do-it-yourself guide to psychoanalysis. I couldn't and didn't deal with deep, inner emotions. I have been shamelessly superficial. The very title of the book telegraphs its punch. HOW TO MAKE IT IN A MAN'S WORLD is a playful, irreverent way of saying: this is gamesmanship; this is a matter of external, acquired values; this is just for fun.

I hope that message came through. But whether you adopt that attitude or not, you are more than human if there haven't been times when you agonize over the central problem of the real you versus the you in your job. How can you be true to yourself and still project an effective occupational image? How will you continue to differentiate real values from illusory ones, immediate goals from the long view, empty status from true personal worth?

You've been grilling yourself so mercilessly for so long, it won't hurt to turn on the third degree for just a little bit longer. Answer honestly. First of all—success. Or should I say $uccess. Does it suggest sellout? Does it stand for conformity, money hunger, callousness? Or are you possibly putting it down because you find refuge in failure or because you have become tolerant of mediocrity in a job or because you are really satisfied to be lost in the crowd?

If success is a pleasure word for you, then being successful would be true to the real you. Even though success is not one of life's immutable values. Even though being successful may not be as "good" as being Albert Schweitzer or as good as being a dedicated poet or an unsalaried civil rights worker.

In my own little niche in the world I feel successful and I like it. It spares me from feeling like a failure. It frees me from financial concerns which many women dwell on, married or not. It pleases my ego when I am feeling mousy or excessively self-critical. It's not everything. But it's a nice little extra.

Next question: Do you like excitement? Can you get your kicks from conversations with bright people, from delivering a perfect job, meeting a deadline on the button, having *the* right idea? Then having an exciting, challenging job and doing it well is right for the real you.

My enthusiasms may strike some people as peculiarly eclectic. I'm thrilled by a courageous statement by the U. S. Attorney General on the Fifth Amendment. I'm also thrilled by finding an author who remembers to mention the title of his book when he appears on the "Tonight" show. I'm crazy about my husband for leaving me a funny loving personal letter in my silverware drawer. I'm also crazy about my secretary for collating sixty-five press clippings and packing twenty salesmen's kits in two hours flat.

I've had my name or picture published in *Time*, *Life*, the New York *Times*, the London *Times*, the Manchester *Guardian* and a dozen other publications. In all honesty, none of these milestones produced anywhere near the rapture I felt about my fifth wedding anniversary or the pride I experienced watching my children excel in a dance class. Career landmarks don't supplant private excitements. They can be separate but equal —same as they are for a man.

If you're uncomfortable or guilty about lavishing your enthusiasm on both the ridiculous and the sublime, just ask yourself why. Are you afraid you'll burn yourself out? Peak too soon? Lose your grip on what matters? That's really utter nonsense. Zest is free. And your capacity for it should be like the bottomless jug. In fact, excitement and enthusiasm, rather than exhausting one, are self-nourishing. A zingy day of "insignificant" pleasures on the job makes you more receptive to great theatre or stimulating conversation that night.

On with the third degree. Do you rate glamour as an incentive to better yourself? Are you too *serious* to admit that you like good restaurants, interesting parties, a bright, comfortable, cheerful office? Is there really any intellectual merit to working at a cramped desk in a tiny airless cubicle? In protecting your special you are you ending up in a line with forty-nine other girls who type the same forms you do? Sure, it's great to quote Schopenhauer, sing along with a Wagner opera or know all the biographical details of the Rolling Stones ever since they were little pebbles. But that's in your private life. Wouldn't you like to meet a living, breathing philosopher on a job in the local university? Or escort a real, live tenor to an audition in your capacity as an artist's agent? That's glamour, with a capital "g" and that rhymes with "gee!" and that stands for "Great!"

I'm not ashamed to tell you that I still get fluttery about celebrities, big brains, famous places, political or show-business big shots. Are you ashamed to admit to such "superficial" interests?

If so, then take a leaf from Dr. James B. Conant, a courtly gentleman whom we met at a social gathering. Dr. Conant has been president and president emeritus of Harvard University, chairman of the National Defense Research Committee, a key presidential adviser in three administrations at least, one of the few men Truman consulted on the decision to drop the atomic bomb, a brilliant scientist, educator, author of nearly twenty books, United States High Commissioner and Ambassador to Germany and who knows what else. I was in a state of partial paralysis at sitting beside him and hearing his account of the top-secret Manhattan Project. My sherry sloshed in my glass. My celery stick sounded like the fall of the Roman Empire as I chewed it. I rehearsed all my comments mentally before letting them out. This man was walking, talking history.

The legend turned to me at one point and asked me about myself. I said a sentence or two about my family and told him where I work.

"Oh, isn't Bernard Geis the publisher of *Victory Over Myself?*" he asked.

"Yes, we are," said I, amazed not only that he had time to read anything other than treaties, two-page equations and university charters, but stunned that he mentioned Floyd Patterson's book. Could it be that Dr. James Conant was a heavyweight fight fan?

"Tell me," he said earnestly, "what's Floyd Patterson *really* like?"

To me, Dr. Conant was Big Name incarnate. To Dr. Conant, I was interesting because I knew a boxer he admired but had never met. Glamour is a very democratic quality.

An unabashed celebrity lover is an honest human being. A blasé cool character doesn't fool anyone. He cheats himself of one of life's little pleasures. Glamour is fun. Luxury is nice. Fame is kicks in small doses. The real you can take it without being corrupted, I'm sure.

Next question is one most of us spend a good part of our lives answering: what am I, at heart, a woman or an executive? Because I've had to face up to it, and because a seemingly casual, almost silly experience helped me to do so, and because at the beginning of this book I promised to level with you, here it is for what it's worth.

It's easy to say, "Why, of course, I'm both a woman and an executive." But that's often more in the realm of definition than positive assurance. What if one is confronted with a classic test, such as the one faced by the man whose rowboat capsized and he could save only his wife or his mother?

My experience was much less dramatic. To celebrate the record sales of one of our books, a national magazine sent a photographer to our office to take pictures of the author, my boss and myself. They left it to me to select the picture I liked best to run with the story.

There were only five final poses to choose from. By some quirk of fate all the pictures in which I looked well were unfavorable to Mr. Geis—and vice versa. (Let's forget the poor author; I was worried only about approving either a bad picture of myself or a bad shot of my boss.) To make matters worse, Mr. Geis was out of town and I couldn't pass the buck to him.

What did I do? You may not believe it. I decided to be a complete pro. I selected a photo in which *both* Mr. Geis and the author came off well and I looked simply horrid. And guess what? Not only did I survive but my feminine ego was never more healthy.

This incident marked the point at which I knew that I could stop reassuring myself that I could remain a woman. I could relax. I didn't have to prove anything to anyone any more. A ghastly photograph of me did not in itself strip me of my femininity. I had made a business decision contrary to my female ego interests. But I was still a woman, intact.

Next question: Do you know what you like? If that sounds silly it's only because you haven't thought about the question yet. I have only one friend who really *knows* what she likes. She can go into a rummage sale, run through acres of jumbled, overloaded counters and emerge twenty minutes later with a magnificent beaded purse that's at least one hundred and ten years old. She can review a mountain of travel folders describing Caribbean islands, Mexican mountain retreats and Jet Set watering spots—and in no time flat she *knows* which place is right for her vacation. She knows what she likes in her home, on her table, in her job, in her friends. Some call her rigid and opinionated, but she's not. She's strong and confident about her own capacity for satisfaction.

Are you? Or do you agonize about which dress to buy for an art-show opening; whether cranshaw melon or stuffed avocado is best for your dinner party; which client takes precedence in the clinch for time. Most of us sweat a little over decisions large and small. My absolutely positive friend is a rarity. But too many girls are at the extreme opposite end of the decisiveness spectrum—and I suspect it's partly because so many aren't sure what they like or want.

One girl takes an hour to choose a piece of clothing and invariably *hates* it as soon as she gets it home. Another friend hasn't put a stick of furniture in her house because she's terrified of deciding on the "wrong" things. A third girl never answers a business question the first time she's asked. She invariably says, "I'll think about that and get back to you." Even the most simple questions throw her. She can't decide. She gets all knotted up about what she *really* thinks and what she should say.

This business of right and wrong things to like or do or say or think is a dreadful patch of quicksand. The more you weigh and censor your responses to things, the more you get sucked into dizzying alternatives. Wouldn't it be easier to just like what you like. Don't bother worrying if it's consistent with your "values." Don't panic if you choose to do something which doesn't fit your self-image. Maybe it's the image that's blurred.

You've been pegging yourself as the jaunty, jolly showgirl type, let's say, and suddenly you find that you're mad about doing aerospace research. Do it. You can always turn go-go after hours.

Your duties as advertising director involve certain choices—like the color for the company catalogue, for instance. You're faced with cerise, lavender, periwinkle, mauve, beige and crimson—and you don't know what you like. The paper samples are spread before you like a drunken rainbow. The lavender is lovely but you think they'll think your feminine bias is showing. The beige is drab but maybe they'll like you for showing sensible conservatism. The crimson is too flashy for your vice president's tastes. Cerise is no better. Mauve is too much like last year's catalogue color—they'll think you can't be original. The periwinkle blue is pretty but how can you be sure? This kind of torture causes ulcers. If you are in the habit of such self-inflicted punishment try flipping a coin to get you past decision-making crises. And stay after work to write one hundred times over: there is no absolute right and wrong. . . . There is no absolute right and wrong. . . . Remember what I told you about that negative editorial report on *Gone With the Wind*.

You are just as capable as the next person of having an opinion and sticking to it. Your opinion has just as good a chance of being the best one. Your instinctual tastes *can* operate on a job. You don't have to be rigid. But you can know what you like if you just let go. And *do* what you like if you can surmount the eternal hang-up of measuring your acts against some fiction about the real you.

The real you is whatever you are at any given moment. I am a confessed chameleon, myself. Sometimes I see myself as a little girl. I need help. Someone to protect me. Someone to assure me. At other times I feel like a blazing amazon, carrying the load of worldly woes, office worries, home responsibilities—invincible, indestructible, solid. Some days I'm a flaming phony. I cajole disconsolate authors when I really feel like telling them, "Your book isn't selling because it isn't a great book—not because there was a blizzard and no one could get to a bookstore." Other times I'm honest to the point of pain. "CBS News canceled you because the invasion of Czechoslovakia is a helluva lot more important than your book."

To me, the phony is as "real" as the honest woman. Or, to put it more generally, the surface is as real as the contents.

I didn't come by this conclusion independently. A long-ago lecture by Mark Van Doren caused my conversion. The philosophy of this poet-professor may be paraphrased in this way: we are not who we think we are but the way we behave and the way others see us. Don't fall into the pit of certainty. We never really know what we think until we've heard what we've said. We think we understand something if we put a name to it. But there aren't always reasons, labels or explanations. That is why we must admire superficiality. Think again about the old saying: beauty is only skin deep. How often are we allowed any deeper access to someone than his surface. We are really all the same beneath that skin. The surface is what differentiates us. It is more important to accept others and ourselves than to understand.

Van Doren's poetic philosophy is an echo of an essential Zen Buddhist precept: be interested not in what I am or who I am but in the act of doing and being.

Isn't that what the real you should be concerned with? Doing and being. Not should I? Or is it really me?

I hope you don't feel that it's ludicrous to talk in philosophical terms about the question of whether or not to make it in a man's world. As long as that step looms for a woman as a major life choice and not just an easy route to take any old time, the point *does* have relevance.

In talking to dozens of women who have considered the question of "what it all means," I myself have learned a lot about individual doing and being. About adjustment. And self-acceptance.

A computer specialist said that she realized that what she did for a living had nothing to do with the real world. "My labors only increase the company's profits," she reasoned. "It's that kind of a dead end. It has nothing to do with humanitarian improvement. I don't ever kid myself that what I'm doing is important. I do it for the entertainment of getting ahead. I know that teaching would be important. It would *help* people. But if I wanted to teach I would be a teacher. Long ago I realized that I'd rather play at being an executive than contribute to the world. If I abandoned my job for something more "meaningful" then I'd really be a phony. Why should something pleasurable always cause guilt? I don't feel guilty about the pleasure I receive from a nonmeaningful endeavor. Not everyone can help the world. I'm not selfish. I just do my helping privately and on my own time."

That kind of outspoken honesty is food for thought. In fact, it's a banquet. You may not like that girl's truth in its unadorned state. But I admire her a whole lot more than the kind of woman who says she's saving money to adopt a Korean orphan while you and I see her in a new fur coat every season, lapping up her career success without a glance toward Korea.

A lovely, feminine journalist says about making it in a man's world: "I value straightforwardness and I despise conniving. The business world allows me to be me, fair and square. It operates as a 'you get what you give' operation. It satisfies my sense of order. I know very well that there is very little meaningful work done on this planet. What I do is meaningful in microcosm. I am honest in my writing—though I may not write about cosmic issues. I think it's axiomatic that we all want to learn as much as possible in a lifetime. I feel I'm learning. My job expands me. It gives me a chance to see a completely new set of relationships. For example, perverse as it may sound, I find it fascinating to discover that people can be afraid of me. Writers get nervous at meeting me. Because I'm their editor. They're not nervous because I'm little Sally Smith. Learning about people and their reactions is something I want out of life."

An interesting assessment of herself was offered by a magazine editor, who by all lights is sitting pretty. She says: "I'm doing a job that makes me feel alive and kicking. But I consider myself an absolute failure. I'm a realistic failure, though. And a successful failure. I've known for a long time that I don't have it in me to become what I really want to be. But knowing that I want it and will never do it is enough for me. In the last analysis, my work makes me happy. Even though I'm an absolute failure. You see, I *could* be ecstatic. But happy will have to do."

A publicity expert tried to describe the fine line between the real and the manufactured personality. "In the beginning of my working experience I remember practicing to look self-confident. I knew I needed it to survive. The exact moment when the pose became the person, I can't tell you. At some point though, the appearance of self-confidence and calm and assured efficiency deepened until it became natural. Illusion became reality through practice. I don't feel any more of a phony for having smoothed my rough edges than the average woman feels phony for tweezing her overgrown eyebrows."

Another magazine executive compared herself with her best friend: "She's involved up to her ears in the Peace Movement. She really works on the inside and is intensely involved with disarmament efforts, nuclear test-ban agreements and protest marches. I envy her because her job and her personal values are perfectly merged. But is she content? Not a chance. She's peeved because she puts in long hours at half the pay I receive. She's furious at the intramovement politics and backbiting. She'd like to be in my shoes—making good money, doing something diverting and saving her real energies for extracurricular "revolutionary" work. She made me realize that you can't wear a hair shirt for wanting to make somebody of yourself. You *can* please yourself and others without guilt and without being a sacrificial lamb to an ideology."

A publishing executive who has enjoyed a meteoric rise had this to contribute: "I'm the same me as I was six months ago when I was a secretary. But now my status precedes me into a room. My title is what people meet for lunch, not me. And that suits me fine. Because I know who's behind the title. Just as I knew who was behind the secretary. Same girl. Different label. There are three stages: the fact of my changed status; people reacting to it; and finally my reacting to their reactions. And now that is the reality. I don't feel uncomfortable with it."

This same girl had a theory about the career-prone breed of woman: "Lots of us were stars when we were young. You get used to being the brightest girl in your neighborhood or the pride of the family. Daddy brings home the bacon. You bring home the As. Certain facets of your personality become over-developed. Achievement is our keynote. It's what drives us and as long as we live we're out to get As.

"With the help of an analyst I now realize that this 'A' syn-drome is an escape. The reward becomes the only goal. I used to function for it. Through a recent death very close to me I've become quite an existentialist. I see that we're all here for such a short time. You can't get people to stop long enough to read your insides. You may as well have an 'A' outside as a 'C-plus.' You may as well be known as a success than as a failure. As long as the voice inside tells you that what matters is caring about people and being cared for. All this floss, this zapping onward and upward is fine in its place. But I don't expect them to put on my gravestone: 'Here lies a terrific little worker.' I want them to say 'Beloved wife and mother' and my working life can never determine that one way or another."

Whatever your lifelong itinerary, wherever your career or business vicissitudes take you, however you choose to search for your essence, remember one thing: you take yourself with you wherever you go. Like yourself, respect yourself, enjoy yourself and accept yourself. And if you feel the real you, or any you, slipping into self-doubt or veering from your course into par-oxysms of inner probing just think of these words from a column entitled "Let the Real You Alone" by New York *Times* satirist, Russell Baker:

"The psychiatric fad these days is 'identity.' Walk into any

room full of strangers, lift a glass and two swallows later some
sadist whose pleasure derives from slashing other persons' egos
will be telling you, 'The trouble with you is that you don't know
who you really are.'

"Knowing 'who you really are' is supposed, for reasons that
no one can persuasively explain, to be essential to putting one's
life in order. Those who do not know are said to be caught in
the dreadful 'identity crisis.'

"It is hard to conceive of a more fallacious doctrine. For the
average person nothing but the most abject depression can result from the sudden discovery of who he or she really is.

"It is enough for him to discover, in the nick of time, who he
isn't. His answer to any tormentor who threatens to tell him
who he actually is should be 'If you do so, I shall never be
able to forgive you.'"

Whether you have been tormentor or tormented, existentialist
or Zen Buddhist, an 'A' person or a 'C-plus' person, you're here
now for a pat on the back and you're going to get it. What I
really should offer is a pat on the backside and a push out the
door. That I'll leave to someone closer to you than the pages of
this book.

Between you and me there is a special one-to-one relationship. You know my background, my limitations, my satisfactions
with the route that I chose for myself. All I know about you is
that you've come this far with me and that's all I have to know.
You want something more than what you have. You need something different than what satisfies most women. Only one woman
in two thousand makes it to a real executive position. And the
ratio zooms out of sight when you count how many of those at
the top find all-round happiness—privately, publicly and professionally. But *you* are going to be one of those chosen few.

You *can* be a spirited, fulfilled, satisfied, accomplished female all rolled into one pretty package. Please don't let anyone tell you that it's either/or. Happiness comes from all directions.

The man's world is full of men who like women—and *you* they'll be crazy about. Make it big in whatever field you like best. Draw a grandiose mental blueprint for yourself, stake out your property, subcontract the job of self-improvement where necessary, lay a sound foundation and then pour the concrete. Don't get tangled up in role definition or femininity tremors. Just go.